EVERYMAN,
I WILL GO WITH THEE
AND BE THY GUIDE,
IN THY MOST NEED
TO GO BY THY SIDE

ENGLISH ROMANTIC POETS

••••••••••••••••••••

EDITED BY
JONATHAN BATE

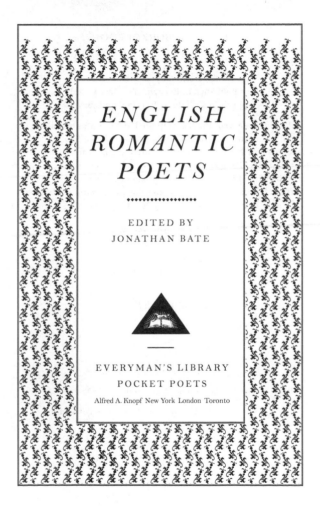

EVERYMAN'S LIBRARY
POCKET POETS

Alfred A. Knopf New York London Toronto

THIS IS A BORZOI BOOK
PUBLISHED BY ALFRED A. KNOPF

This selection by Jonathan Bate
first published in Everyman's Library, 2022
Copyright © 2022 by Everyman's Library

everymanslibrary.com
www.everymanslibrary.co.uk

ISBN 978-0-593-53552-3 (US)
978-1-84159-826-0 (UK)

A CIP catalogue record for this book is available
from the British Library

Typography by Peter B. Willberg

Book design by Barbara de Wilde and Carol Devine Carson

Typeset in the UK by Input Data Services Ltd,
Isle Abbotts, Somerset

Printed and bound in Germany
by GGP Media GmbH, Pössneck

CONTENTS

INFLUENCE OF NATURAL OBJECTS

INTIMATIONS OF MORTALITY AND
    IMMORTALITY

INTRODUCTION

Jean-Jacques Rousseau laid many of the intellectual foundations for the French Revolution, but an even profounder legacy was his influence on the great shift in cultural mood that we call the Romantic movement. After Rousseau, it became acceptable for a grown man to cry, for powdered wigs to be thrown away, and for a young woman to sport a diaphanous figure-hugging chemise. It was the age of 'sensibility' as opposed to 'sense'. Where the French revolutionaries had their declaration of the rights of man, the English paid more attention to J. W. von Goethe's romantic and Rousseau-esque novel, *The Sorrows of Young Werther*, which a contemporary critic splendidly described as 'a declaration of the rights of feeling'.

In 1798, under the imprint of a minor provincial publisher, a slender volume of poetry was published with no author's name on the cover and the unassuming title, *Lyrical Ballads, with a few other poems.* Twenty years later it was recognized as the point of ignition for English literature's revolution of sensibility. The great essayist William Hazlitt looked back on his first acquaintance with the two authors, the as yet little-known William Wordsworth and Samuel Taylor Coleridge, as an epoch in his life. As they read aloud from the collection, Hazlitt felt 'The sense of a new style and a new spirit in poetry ... It had to me something of the effect that arises from the turning up of the fresh soil, or of the first welcome breath of Spring.'

The literary establishment did not share Hazlitt's enthusiasm. The lukewarm reception of *Lyrical Ballads* led Wordsworth to write a preface when the collection was reissued together with a second volume of new poems. It was his manifesto for the new poetry of feeling.

His aim, he said, had been to explore 'the manner in which we associate ideas in a state of excitement', to examine how human beings behave at times of extreme emotional stress. In particular, he had sought to tap into some of the fundamental passions which the urbane and polished poetry of the previous century had all too often neglected: the love of nature, the memory of childhood, righteous indignation at poverty and the slave trade. 'Poetry is the spontaneous overflow of powerful feelings,' he wrote, 'it takes its origin from emotion recollected in tranquillity'. The medium of verse enabled poets to express and order those strong emotions.

This anthology includes a wide range of Words-worth's greatest poems – on childhood, nature, mourning – as well as Coleridge's exquisite meditation on fatherhood, 'Frost at Midnight', the first half of his immortal 'Ancient Mariner', and the mysterious fragment 'Kubla Khan' (allegedly composed in an opium dream interrupted by the knock on the door of 'a person from Porlock'). It also looks before and after: back to William Cowper, whose blank verse in the 1780s paved the way for Wordsworth and Coleridge, and to the seemingly simple but eerily profound *Songs of Innocence and of Experience* by the visionary printmaker William Blake, then forward to the younger generation of Romantics – John Keats, Percy Shelley, Felicia Hemans – who fell under the spell of Wordsworth, but reacted with dismay as he veered to the political right.

It also introduces the reader to some lesser-known voices, such as two women greatly admired by Wordsworth: Helen Maria Williams, who combined poetry of 'sensibility' with eyewitness reporting of the revolution in Paris, and Charlotte Smith, a key figure in the revival of the sonnet form and the author of 'Beachy Head', extolling the glories of landscape and sea. Coleridge, meanwhile, was full of praise for the genius of Mary Robinson, who worked with him as poetry editor for a newspaper. She had an eventful life as a teenage bride, Shakespearean actress, royal mistress, fashion icon, feminist pamphleteer, woman overcoming disability, novelist and poet. She memorably portrayed a feral child discovered in rural France as a Rousseauesque 'noble savage'.

Though Romanticism was a pan-European movement, this anthology gathers its *English* poetic contributors, including a handful of Celtic figures whose writing had great influence on the London literary scene – Robert Burns, the pioneering rural working-class poet; Sir Walter Scott, master of historical narrative poetry (which he would eventually abandon in favour of the novel); and the Irishman Tom Moore, who became Lord Byron's biographer despite being in the room with publisher John Murray when the fatal decision was made to burn his scandalous memoirs.

It was with Byron's long travel poem *Childe Harold's Pilgrimage* that, as he put it, he awoke and found himself famous. He reached the peak of his skill in the comic epic *Don Juan*. For the most part it is a romping anti-Romantic journey, but the union of shipwrecked Juan and beautiful Haidée, included here, is as romantic-with-a-small-r as imaginable.

We think of the Romantic artist as a solitary figure, eking out a living in a garret or wandering lonely as a cloud, but in fact the poets of the age were highly collaborative. Coleridge worked closely with the other 'Lake Poet' Robert Southey, while Wordsworth's writing was intimately bound to the exquisite journals of his sister Dorothy (an occasional poet herself). Keats was heavily reliant on poet and publisher Leigh Hunt. One evening they sat down together to write competing sonnets on the subject of 'The Grasshopper and the Cricket', just as Shelley and his friend Horace Smith both wrote sonnets on the fragments of an ancient statue in the desert – the origin of 'Ozymandias'. And it was Shelley who created the myth that Keats was killed in the prime of his youth not only by tuberculosis but also by the cruelty of his critics. The elegy *Adonais* endures as the exemplary anthem for genius doomed to die young: it is still possible to see a video clip of Mick Jagger quoting it in memory of his Rolling Stones colleague Brian Jones during a Hyde Park rock concert in 1969.

Sometimes, however, the Romantic poet cuts a lonely figure. Letitia Landon, who published under the initials L. E. L. and was branded as the female Byron, died from an overdose of prussic acid (accident, suicide?) far away on the Gold Coast of Africa. She is represented here by a Lake District waterfall poem and an improvisation on *Romeo and Juliet*, typical of the age's obsession with Shakespeare. Most poignant of all is John Clare, the 'Northamptonshire Peasant Poet', who spent the last twenty-four years of his life confined in a lunatic asylum. The full range of his achievement is sampled in this selection: from the lost love of early years to delicate sketches of birds and nests to seasonal scenes to protests over the enclosure of the landscape and the oppression of the poor to laments for his alienation from his home and ultimately the fracturing of his mind in mental illness. For a long time, Blake, Wordsworth, Coleridge, Keats, Shelley and Byron were thought of as the 'major' Romantic poets. Clare is at last recognized as more than their equal: he is England's greatest poet of the observation of the natural world, a man whose ecological vision of our bond with the earth speaks with special power to our own age of environmental fragility.*

Jonathan Bate

---

* Poets usually left punctuation and layout to their publishers, none more so than Clare. This edition is deliberately eclectic in its conventions of capitalization, punctuation and whether or not to elide unstressed past participles as 'd: sometimes original manuscripts are followed, with light editing; at other times, the early printed texts. Asterisks indicate a gap where discrete sections of long poems are included.

CHILDHOOD

CHILDHOOD

O dear to us ever the scenes of our childhood,
The green spots we played in, the school where we met,
The heavy old desk where we thought of the
     wildwood,
Where we pored o'er the sums which the master had set.
I loved the old church-school, both inside and outside,
I loved the dear ash trees and sycamore too,
The graves where the buttercups burning gold
     outvied
And the spire where pellitory dangled and grew,

The bees i' the wall that were flying about
The thistles, the henbane and mallows all day,
And crept in their holes when the sun had gone out
And the butterfly ceased on the blossoms to play.
O, dear is the round stone upon the green hill,
The pinfold hoof-printed with oxen – and bare,
The old princess-feather tree growing there still
And the swallows and martins wheeling round in
     the air

Where the chaff whipping outward lodges round the
     barn door
And the dunghill cock struts with his hens in the rear
And sings 'Cockadoodle' full twenty times o'er

And then claps his wings as he'd fly in the air;
And there's the old cross with its round-about steps
And the weathercock creaking quite round in the
        wind,
And there's the old hedge with its glossy red hips
Where the green-linnet's nest I have hurried to find –

To be in time for the school or before the bell rung.
There's the odd martin's nest o'er the shoemaker's
        door;
On the shoemaker's chimney the old swallows sung
That had built and sung there in the season before;
Then we went to seek pooties among the old furze
On the heaths, in the meadows beside the deep lake,
And returned with torn clothes all covered wi' burs
And oh, what a row my fond mother would make!

Then to play boiling kettles just by the yard door,
Seeking out for short sticks and a bundle of straw;
Bits of pots stand for teacups after sweeping the floor
And the children are placed under school-mistress's
        awe;
There's one set for pussy, another for doll,
And for butter and bread they'll each nibble a haw,
And on a great stone as a table they loll,
The finest small tea party ever you saw.

The stiles we rode upon 'all a cock-horse',
The mile-a-minute swee
On creaking gates, the stools o' moss —
What happy seats had we!
There's nought can compare to the days of our
    childhood:
The mole-hills like sheep in a pen
Where the clodhopper sings like the bird in the
    wildwood,
All forget us before we are men.

THERE WAS A BOY

There was a boy, ye knew him well, ye cliffs
And islands of Winander! many a time,
At evening, when the stars had just begun
To move along the edges of the hills,
Rising or setting, would he stand alone,
Beneath the trees, or by the glimmering lake,
And there, with fingers interwoven, both hands
Press'd closely palm to palm and to his mouth
Uplifted, he, as through an instrument,
Blew mimic hootings to the silent owls
That they might answer him. And they would shout
Across the wat'ry vale and shout again,
Responsive to his call, with quivering peals,
And long halloos, and screams, and echoes loud
Redoubled and redoubled, a wild scene
Of mirth and jocund din. And, when it chanced
That pauses of deep silence mock'd his skill,
Then, sometimes, in that silence, while he hung
Listening, a gentle shock of mild surprise
Has carried far into his heart the voice
Of mountain torrents, or the visible scene
Would enter unawares into his mind
With all its solemn imagery, its rocks,
Its woods, and that uncertain heaven, receiv'd
Into the bosom of the steady lake.

Fair are the woods, and beauteous is the spot,
The vale where he was born: the church-yard hangs
Upon a slope above the village school,
And there along that bank when I have pass'd
At evening, I believe, that near his grave
A full half-hour together I have stood,
Mute – for he died when he was ten years old.

EVENING SCHOOLBOYS

Harken that happy shout – the schoolhouse door
Is open thrown and out the younkers teem
Some run to leap-frog on the rushy moor
And others dabble in the shallow stream
Catching young fish and turning pebbles o'er
For mussel clams – Look in that mellow gleam
Where the retiring sun that rests the while
Streams through the broken hedge – How happy seem
Those schoolboy friendships leaning o'er the stile
Both reading in one book – anon a dream
Rich with new joys doth their young hearts beguile
And the book's pocketed most hastily
Ah happy boys well may ye turn and smile
When joys are yours that never cost a sigh.

INFANT JOY
(*Song of Innocence*)

I have no name
I am but two days old –
What shall I call thee?
I happy am
Joy is my name,–
Sweet joy befall thee!

Pretty joy!
Sweet joy but two days old,
Sweet joy I call thee;
Thou dost smile.
I sing the while
Sweet joy befall thee.

WILLIAM BLAKE

INFANT SORROW
(*Song of Experience*)

My mother groan'd! my father wept.
Into the dangerous world I leapt:
Helpless, naked, piping loud:
Like a fiend hid in a cloud.

Struggling in my father's hands:
Striving against my swaddling bands:
Bound and weary I thought best
To sulk upon my mother's breast.

HOLY THURSDAY
(*Song of Innocence*)

'Twas on a Holy Thursday their innocent faces clean
The children walking two & two in red & blue
    & green
Grey-headed beadles walk'd before with wands as
    white as snow
Till into the high dome of Paul's they like Thames
    waters flow

O what a multitude they seem'd these flowers of
    London town
Seated in companies they sit with radiance all their own
The hum of multitudes was there but multitudes
    of lambs
Thousands of little boys & girls raising their innocent
    hands

Now like a mighty wind they raise to heaven the voice
    of song
Or like harmonious thunderings the seats of heaven
    among
Beneath them sit the aged men wise guardians of
    the poor
Then cherish pity, lest you drive an angel from
    your door.

WILLIAM BLAKE

HOLY THURSDAY
(*Song of Experience*)

Is this a holy thing to see,
In a rich and fruitful land,
Babes reduc'd to misery,
Fed with cold and usurous hand?

Is that trembling cry a song?
Can it be a song of joy?
And so many children poor?
It is a land of poverty!

And their sun does never shine.
And their fields are bleak and bare.
And their ways are fill'd with thorns.
It is eternal winter there.

For where'er the sun does shine,
And where'er the rain does fall:
Babe can never hunger there,
Nor poverty the mind appall.

THE CHIMNEY SWEEPER
(*Song of Experience*)

A little black thing among the snow:
Crying 'weep! weep!' in notes of woe!
'Where are thy father and mother? say?'
'They are both gone up to the church to pray.

Because I was happy upon the heath,
And smil'd among the winter's snow,
They clothed me in the clothes of death,
And taught me to sing the notes of woe.

And because I am happy and dance and sing,
They think they have done me no injury:
And are gone to praise God and his Priest and King,
Who make up a heaven of our misery.'

WILLIAM BLAKE   29

THE SAVAGE OF AVEYRON

The story first suggested itself to her after perusing various accounts of a SAVAGE BOY, lately discovered in the Forest of Aveyron, in the department of Tarn, and said to be then existing at Paris.

'Twas in the mazes of a wood,
The lonely wood of Aveyron,
I heard a melancholy tone,
It seem'd to freeze my blood!
A torrent near was flowing fast,
And hollow was the morning blast,
As o'er the leafless woods it past,
While terror-fraught I stood!
O! mazy woods of Aveyron!
O! wilds of dreary solitude!
Amid thy thorny alleys rude
I thought myself alone!
I thought no living thing could be
So weary of the world as me,
While on my winding path the pale moon shone.

Sometimes the tone was loud and sad,
And sometimes dulcet, faint, and slow;
And then a tone of frantic woe,
It almost made me mad.
The burthen was 'alone! alone!'
And then the heart did feebly groan,
Then suddenly a cheerful tone
Proclaimed a spirit glad!
O! mazy woods of Aveyron!
O! wilds of dreary solitude!
Amid your thorny alleys rude
I wish'd myself – a traveller alone!

'Alone!' I heard the wild boy say,
And swift he climb'd a blasted oak,
And there, while morning's herald woke,
He watch'd the opening day.
Yet dark and sunken was his eye,
Like a lorn maniac's, wild and shy,
And scowling like a winter sky,
Without one beaming ray!
Then, mazy woods of Aveyron,
Then, wilds of dreary solitude,
Amid thy thorny alleys rude
I sigh'd to be – a traveller alone!

'Alone! Alone!' I heard him shriek,
'Twas like the shriek of dying man!
And then to mutter he began,
But, O! *he could not speak!*
I saw him point to heaven, and sigh,
The big drop trembled in his eye,
And slowly from the yellow sky,
I saw the pale moon break:
I saw the woods of Aveyron,
Their wilds of dreary solitude!
I mark'd their thorny alleys rude,
And wish'd to be a traveller alone!

His hair was long and black, and he
From infancy *alone* had been!
For since his fifth year he had seen
None mark'd his destiny!
No mortal ear had heard his groan,
For him no beam of hope had shone,
While sad he sigh'd – 'alone, alone!'
Beneath the blasted tree.
And there, O! woods of Aveyron!
O! wilds of dreary solitude!
Amid your thorny alleys rude,
I thought myself a traveller alone.

And now upon the blasted tree
He carved three notches, broad and long,
And all the while he sang a song
Of Nature's melody!
And though of words he little knew,
And though his dulcet tones were few,
Across the yielding bark he drew,
Deep sighing, notches three.
O! mazy woods of Aveyron!
O! wilds of dreary solitude,
Amid your thorny alleys rude
Upon this blasted oak, no sun shone!

And now he pointed, one, two, three,
And now he shriek'd with wild dismay!
And now he paced the thorny way,
Quitting the blasted tree.
It was a dark December morn,
The dew was frozen on the thorn,
But to a wretch so sad, so lorn,
All days alike would be!
Yet, mazy woods of Aveyron!
Yet, wilds of dreary solitude!
Amid your frosty alleys rude,
I wish'd to be a traveller alone!

I follow'd him along the wood,
To a small grot his hands had made,
Deep in a black rock's sullen shade,
Beside a tumbling flood!
Upon the earth I saw him spread
Of wither'd leaves a narrow bed,
Yellow as gold, and streak'd with red,
They look'd like streaks of blood!
Fall'n from the woods of Aveyron,
And scatter'd o'er the solitude
By midnight whirlwinds, strong and rude,
To pillow the scorch'd brain, that throbb'd alone.

Wild berries were his winter food,
With them his sallow lip was dyed!
On chestnuts wild he fed beside,
Steep'd in the foamy flood.
Chequer'd with scars his breast was seen,
Wounds streaming fresh with anguish keen,
And marks where other wounds had been
Torn by the brambles rude.
Such was the boy of Aveyron,
The tenant of that solitude,
Where still by misery unsubdu'd,
He wander'd nine long winters, all alone!

Before the step of his rude throne,
The squirrel sported, tame and gay;
The dormouse slept its life away,
Nor heard his midnight groan:
About his form a garb he wore,
Ragged it was, and mark'd with gore,
And yet, whene'er 'twas folded o'er,
Full many a spangle shone!
Like little stars, O! Aveyron,
They gleam'd amid thy solitude,
Or like, along thy alleys rude,
The summer dew-drops sparkling in the sun!

It once had been a lady's vest,
White as the whitest mountain snow,
Till ruffian hands had taught to flow
The fountain of her breast!
Remembrance bade the wild boy trace
Her beauteous form, her angel face,
Her eye that beam'd with heavenly grace,
Her fainting voice that blest,
When in the woods of Aveyron,
Deep in their deepest solitude,
Three barb'rous ruffians shed her blood,
And mock'd, with cruel taunts, her dying groan.

Remembrance trac'd the summer bright,
When all the trees were fresh and green,
When lost, the alleys long between,
The lady pass'd the night;
She pass'd the night bewilder'd wild,
She pass'd it with her fearless child,
Who rais'd his little arms and smil'd
To see the morning light!
While in the woods of Aveyron,
Beneath the broad oak's canopy,
She mark'd aghast the ruffians three,
Waiting to seize the traveller alone!

Beneath the broad oak's canopy
The lovely lady's bones were laid;
But since that hour no breeze has play'd
About the blasted tree!
The leaves all wither'd ere the sun
His next day's rapid course had run,
And ere the summer day was done
It winter seem'd to be!
And still, O! woods of Aveyron,
Amid thy dreary solitude
The oak, a sapless trunk, has stood,
To mark the spot where murder foul was done!

From her the wild boy learnt 'alone,'
She tried to say, 'my babe will die';
But angels caught her parting sigh,
The babe her dying tone.
And from that hour the boy has been
Lord of the solitary scene,
Winding the dreary shades between,
Making his dismal moan!
Till, mazy woods of Aveyron,
Dark wilds of dreary solitude,
Amid your thorny alleys rude,
I thought myself alone;
And could a wretch more wretched be,
More wild and fancy-fraught, than he,
Whose melancholy tale would pierce an heart
        of stone?

CASABIANCA

Young Casabianca, a boy about thirteen years old, son to the admiral of the Orient, remained at his post (in the Battle of the Nile), after the ship had taken fire, and all the guns had been abandoned; and perished in the explosion of the vessel, when the flames had reached the powder.

The boy stood on the burning deck
   Whence all but he had fled;
The flame that lit the battle's wreck
   Shone round him o'er the dead.

Yet beautiful and bright he stood,
   As born to rule the storm;
A creature of heroic blood,
   A proud, though child-like form.

The flames rolled on – he would not go
   Without his Father's word;
That father, faint in death below,
   His voice no longer heard.

He called aloud – 'Say, father, say
   If yet my task is done?'
He knew not that the chieftain lay
   Unconscious of his son.

'Speak, father!' once again he cried,
   'If I may yet be gone!

And' – but the booming shots replied,
   And fast the flames roll'd on.

Upon his brow he felt their breath,
   And in his waving hair;
And look'd from that lone post of death
   In still, yet brave despair.

And shouted but once more aloud,
   'My father! must I stay?'
While o'er him fast, through sail and shroud,
   The wreathing fires made way.

They wrapt the ship in splendour wild,
   They caught the flag on high,
And stream'd above the gallant child,
   Like banners in the sky.

There came a burst of thunder sound –
   The boy – oh! where was he?
– Ask of the winds that far around
   With fragments strewed the sea!

With mast, and helm, and pennon fair,
   That well had borne their part –
But the noblest thing that perish'd there,
   Was that young faithful heart.

SONNET: TO THE RIVER OTTER

Dear native brook! wild streamlet of the West!
How many various-fated years have pass'd,
What happy and what mournful hours, since last
I skimm'd the smooth thin stone along thy breast,
Numbering its light leaps! Yet so deep impress'd
Sink the sweet scenes of childhood, that mine eyes
I never shut amid the sunny ray,
But straight with all their tints thy waters rise,
Thy crossing plank, thy marge with willows grey,
And bedded sand that, vein'd with various dyes,
Gleam'd through thy bright transparence! On my way,
Visions of childhood! oft have ye beguil'd
Lone manhood's cares, yet waking fondest sighs:
Ah! that once more I were a careless child!

MEMORY

from THE WINTER EVENING

Me oft has fancy ludicrous and wild
Sooth'd with a waking dream of houses, towers,
Trees, churches, and strange visages express'd
In the red cinders, while with poring eye
I gazed, myself creating what I saw.
Nor less amused, have I quiescent watch'd
The sooty films that play upon the bars
Pendulous, and foreboding in the view
Of superstition prophesying still
Though still deceived, some stranger's near approach.
'Tis thus the understanding takes repose
In indolent vacuity of thought,
And sleeps and is refresh'd. Meanwhile the face
Conceals the mood lethargic with a mask
Of deep deliberation, as the man
Were task'd to his full strength, absorb'd and lost.
Thus oft reclined at ease, I lose an hour
At evening, till at length the freezing blast,
That sweeps the bolted shutter, summons home
The recollected powers, and, snapping short
The glassy threads with which the fancy weaves
Her brittle toys, restores me to myself.

WILLIAM COWPER   43

FROST AT MIDNIGHT

The Frost performs its secret ministry,
Unhelped by any wind. The owlet's cry
Came loud – and hark, again! loud as before.
The inmates of my cottage, all at rest,
Have left me to that solitude, which suits
Abstruser musings: save that at my side
My cradled infant slumbers peacefully.
'Tis calm indeed! so calm, that it disturbs
And vexes meditation with its strange
And extreme silentness. Sea, hill, and wood,
This populous village! Sea, and hill, and wood,
With all the numberless goings-on of life,
Inaudible as dreams! the thin blue flame
Lies on my low-burnt fire, and quivers not;
Only that film, which fluttered on the grate,
Still flutters there, the sole unquiet thing.
Methinks, its motion in this hush of nature
Gives it dim sympathies with me who live,
Making it a companionable form,
Whose puny flaps and freaks the idling Spirit
By its own moods interprets, every where
Echo or mirror seeking of itself,
And makes a toy of Thought.

                       But O! how oft,
How oft, at school, with most believing mind,

Presageful, have I gazed upon the bars,
To watch that fluttering *stranger*! and as oft
With unclosed lids, already had I dreamt
Of my sweet birth-place, and the old church-tower,
Whose bells, the poor man's only music, rang
From morn to evening, all the hot Fair-day,
So sweetly, that they stirred and haunted me
With a wild pleasure, falling on mine ear
Most like articulate sounds of things to come!
So gazed I, till the soothing things, I dreamt,
Lulled me to sleep, and sleep prolonged my dreams!
And so I brooded all the following morn,
Awed by the stern preceptor's face, mine eye
Fixed with mock study on my swimming book:
Save if the door half opened, and I snatched
A hasty glance, and still my heart leaped up,
For still I hoped to see the *stranger's* face,
Townsman, or aunt, or sister more beloved,
My play-mate when we both were clothed alike!

Dear Babe, that sleepest cradled by my side,
Whose gentle breathings, heard in this deep calm,
Fill up the interspersèd vacancies
And momentary pauses of the thought!
My babe so beautiful! it thrills my heart
With tender gladness, thus to look at thee,
And think that thou shalt learn far other lore,

And in far other scenes! For I was reared
In the great city, pent 'mid cloisters dim,
And saw nought lovely but the sky and stars.
But *thou*, my babe! shalt wander like a breeze
By lakes and sandy shores, beneath the crags
Of ancient mountain, and beneath the clouds,
Which image in their bulk both lakes and shores
And mountain crags: so shalt thou see and hear
The lovely shapes and sounds intelligible
Of that eternal language, which thy God
Utters, who from eternity doth teach
Himself in all, and all things in himself.
Great universal Teacher! he shall mould
Thy spirit, and by giving make it ask.

          Therefore all seasons shall be sweet to thee,
Whether the summer clothe the general earth
With greenness, or the redbreast sit and sing
Betwixt the tufts of snow on the bare branch
Of mossy apple-tree, while the nigh thatch
Smokes in the sun-thaw; whether the eave-drops fall
Heard only in the trances of the blast,
Or if the secret ministry of frost
Shall hang them up in silent icicles,
Quietly shining to the quiet Moon.

LINES WRITTEN A FEW MILES ABOVE TINTERN ABBEY, ON REVISITING THE BANKS OF THE WYE, DURING A TOUR, JULY 13, 1798

Five years have past; five summers, with the length
Of five long winters! and again I hear
These waters, rolling from their mountain-springs
With a sweet inland murmur. – Once again
Do I behold these steep and lofty cliffs,
Which on a wild secluded scene impress
Thoughts of more deep seclusion; and connect
The landscape with the quiet of the sky.
The day is come when I again repose
Here, under this dark sycamore, and view
These plots of cottage-ground, these orchard-tufts,
Which, at this season, with their unripe fruits,
Among the woods and copses lose themselves,
Nor, with their green and simple hue, disturb
The wild green landscape. Once again I see
These hedge-rows, hardly hedge-rows, little lines
Of sportive wood run wild; these pastoral farms,
Green to the very door; and wreathes of smoke
Sent up, in silence, from among the trees,
With some uncertain notice, as might seem,
Of vagrant dwellers in the houseless woods,

Or of some hermit's cave, where by his fire
The hermit sits alone.

      Though absent long,
These forms of beauty have not been to me
As is a landscape to a blind man's eye:
But oft, in lonely rooms, and mid the din
Of towns and cities, I have owed to them,
In hours of weariness, sensations sweet,
Felt in the blood, and felt along the heart,
And passing even into my purer mind
With tranquil restoration: – feelings too
Of unremembered pleasure; such, perhaps,
As may have had no trivial influence
On that best portion of a good man's life,
His little, nameless, unremembered acts
Of kindness and of love. Nor less, I trust,
To them I may have owed another gift,
Of aspect more sublime; that blessed mood,
In which the burthen of the mystery,
In which the heavy and the weary weight
Of all this unintelligible world
Is lighten'd:– that serene and blessed mood,
In which the affections gently lead us on,
Until, the breath of this corporeal frame
And even the motion of our human blood
Almost suspended, we are laid asleep

In body, and become a living soul:
While with an eye made quiet by the power
Of harmony, and the deep power of joy,
We see into the life of things.

                              If this
Be but a vain belief, yet, oh! how oft,
In darkness, and amid the many shapes
Of joyless daylight; when the fretful stir
Unprofitable, and the fever of the world,
Have hung upon the beatings of my heart,
How oft, in spirit, have I turned to thee,
O sylvan Wye! thou wanderer thro' the woods,
How often has my spirit turned to thee!

And now, with gleams of half-extinguish'd thought,
With many recognitions dim and faint,
And somewhat of a sad perplexity,
The picture of the mind revives again:
While here I stand, not only with the sense
Of present pleasure, but with pleasing thoughts
That in this moment there is life and food
For future years. And so I dare to hope,
Though changed, no doubt, from what I was
        when first
I came among these hills; when like a roe
I bounded o'er the mountains, by the sides

Of the deep rivers, and the lonely streams,
Wherever nature led; more like a man
Flying from something that he dreads, than one
Who sought the thing he loved. For nature then
(The coarser pleasures of my boyish days
And their glad animal movements all gone by)
To me was all in all.— I cannot paint
What then I was. The sounding cataract
Haunted me like a passion: the tall rock,
The mountain, and the deep and gloomy wood,
Their colours and their forms, were then to me
An appetite: a feeling and a love,
That had no need of a remoter charm,
By thought supplied, nor any interest
Unborrowed from the eye.— That time is past,
And all its aching joys are now no more,
And all its dizzy raptures. Not for this
Faint I, nor mourn nor murmur: other gifts
Have followed, for such loss, I would believe,
Abundant recompense. For I have learned
To look on nature, not as in the hour
Of thoughtless youth, but hearing oftentimes
The still, sad music of humanity,
Not harsh nor grating, though of ample power
To chasten and subdue. And I have felt
A presence that disturbs me with the joy
Of elevated thoughts; a sense sublime

Of something far more deeply interfused,
Whose dwelling is the light of setting suns,
And the round ocean, and the living air,
And the blue sky, and in the mind of man,
A motion and a spirit, that impels
All thinking things, all objects of all thought,
And rolls through all things. Therefore am I still
A lover of the meadows and the woods,
And mountains; and of all that we behold
From this green earth; of all the mighty world
Of eye, and ear, both what they half-create,
And what perceive; well pleased to recognize
In nature and the language of the sense,
The anchor of my purest thoughts, the nurse,
The guide, the guardian of my heart, and soul
Of all my moral being.

                  Nor perchance,
If I were not thus taught, should I the more
Suffer my genial spirits to decay:
For thou art with me, here, upon the banks
Of this fair river; thou, my dearest Friend,
My dear, dear Friend, and in thy voice I catch
The language of my former heart, and read
My former pleasures in the shooting lights
Of thy wild eyes. Oh! yet a little while
May I behold in thee what I was once,

My dear, dear Sister! and this prayer I make,
Knowing that Nature never did betray
The heart that loved her; 'tis her privilege,
Through all the years of this our life, to lead
From joy to joy: for she can so inform
The mind that is within us, so impress
With quietness and beauty, and so feed
With lofty thoughts, that neither evil tongues,
Rash judgments, nor the sneers of selfish men,
Nor greetings where no kindness is, nor all
The dreary intercourse of daily life,
Shall e'er prevail against us, or disturb
Our cheerful faith, that all which we behold
Is full of blessings. Therefore let the moon
Shine on thee in thy solitary walk;
And let the misty mountain-winds be free
To blow against thee: and in after years,
When these wild ecstasies shall be matured
Into a sober pleasure, when thy mind
Shall be a mansion for all lovely forms,
Thy memory be as a dwelling-place
For all sweet sounds and harmonies; oh! then,
If solitude, or fear, or pain, or grief,
Should be thy portion, with what healing thoughts
Of tender joy wilt thou remember me,
And these my exhortations! Nor, perchance,
If I should be where I no more can hear

Thy voice, nor catch from thy wild eyes these gleams
Of past existence, wilt thou then forget
That on the banks of this delightful stream
We stood together; and that I, so long
A worshipper of Nature, hither came
Unwearied in that service: rather say
With warmer love, oh! with far deeper zeal
Of holier love. Nor wilt thou then forget,
That after many wanderings, many years
Of absence, these steep woods and lofty cliffs,
And this green pastoral landscape, were to me
More dear, both for themselves and for thy sake!

WILLIAM WORDSWORTH   53

from A FAREWELL, FOR TWO YEARS, TO ENGLAND

My native scenes! Can aught in time, or space,
From this fond heart your lov'd remembrance chase?
Link'd to that heart by ties for ever dear,
By Joy's light smile, and Sorrow's tender tear;
By all that ere my anxious hopes employ'd,
By all my soul has suffer'd, or enjoy'd!
Still blended with those well-known scenes, arise
The varying images the past supplies;
The childish sports that fond attention drew,
And charm'd my vacant heart when life was new;
The harmless mirth, the sadness robb'd of power
To cast its shade beyond the present hour –
And that dear hope which sooth'd my youthful breast,
And show'd the op'ning world in beauty dress'd;
That hope which seem'd with bright unfolding rays
(Ah, vainly seem'd!) to gild my future days;
That hope which, early wrapp'd in lasting gloom,
Sunk in the cold inexorable tomb! –
And Friendship, ever powerful to control
The keen emotions of the wounded soul,
To lift the suff'ring spirit from despair,
And bid it feel that life deserves a care.
Still each impression that my heart retains
Is link'd, dear Land! to thee by lasting chains.

REMEMBRANCES

Summer pleasures they are gone like to visions
     every one
& the cloudy days of autumn & of winter cometh on
I tried to call them back but unbidden they are gone
Far away from heart & eye & for ever far away
Dear heart & can it be that such raptures meet decay
I thought them all eternal when by Langley Bush I lay
I thought them joys eternal when I used to shout
     & play
On its bank at 'clink & bandy' 'chock' and 'taw'
     & ducking stone
Where silence sitteth now on the wild heath as
     her own
Like a ruin of the past all alone

When I used to lie & sing by old Eastwell's boiling
     spring
When I used to tie the willow boughs together for
     a 'swing'
& fish with crooked pins & thread & never catch
     a thing
With heart just like a feather – now as heavy as a stone
When beneath old Lea Close Oak I the bottom
     branches broke
To make our harvest cart like so many working folk

& then to cut a straw at the brook to have a soak
O I never dreamed of parting or that trouble had
      a sting
Or that pleasures like a flock of birds would ever take
      to wing
Leaving nothing but a little naked spring

When jumping time away on old Crossberry Way
& eating awes like sugar plumbs ere they had lost
      the may
& skipping like a leveret before the peep of day
On the rolly polly up & downs of pleasant Swordy Well
When in Round Oak's narrow lane as the south got
      black again
We sought the hollow ash that was shelter from
      the rain
With our pockets full of peas we had stolen from
      the grain
How delicious was the dinner time on such a
      show'ry day
O words are poor receipts for what time hath stole away
The ancient pulpit trees & the play

When for school o'er 'Little Field' with its brook
      & wooden brig
Where I swaggered like a man though I was not half
      so big

While I held my little plough though 'twas but a
    willow twig
And drove my team along made of nothing but
    a name
'Gee hep' & 'hoit' & 'woi' – O I never call to mind
These pleasant names of places but I leave a sigh
    behind
While I see the little mouldywarps hang sweeing to
    the wind
On the only aged willow that in all the field remains
& nature hides her face where they're sweeing in their
    chains
& in a silent murmuring complains

Here was commons for the hills where they seek for
    freedom still
Though every commons gone & though traps are set
    to kill
The little homeless miners – O it turns my bosom chill
When I think of old 'Sneap Green' Puddock's Nook &
    Hilly Snow
Where bramble bushes grew & the daisy gemmed
    in dew
& the hills of silken grass like to cushions to the view
When we threw the pismire crumbs when we'd
    nothing else to do
All leveled like a desert by the never weary plough

All vanished like the sun where that cloud is
        passing now
& settled here for ever on its brow

O I never thought that joys would run away from boys
Or that boys would change their minds & forsake such
        summer joys
But alack I never dreamed that the world had
        other toys
To petrify first feelings like the fable into stone
Till I found the pleasure past & a winter come at last
Then the fields were sudden bare & the sky got
        overcast
& boyhoods pleasing haunts like a blossom in
        the blast
Was shrivelled to a withered weed & trampled down
        & done
Till vanished was the morning spring & set that
        summer sun
And winter fought her battle-strife & won

By Langley Bush I roam but the bush hath left its hill
On Cowper Green I stray 'tis a desert strange & chill
& spreading Lea Close Oak ere decay had penned
        its will
To the axe of the spoiler & self-interest fell a prey
& Crossberry Way & Old Round Oak's narrow lane

With its hollow trees like pulpits I shall never
     see again
Inclosure like a Buonaparte let not a thing remain
It levelled every bush & tree & levelled every hill
& hung the moles for traitors – though the brook is
     running still
It runs a naked brook cold & chill

O had I known as then joy had left the paths of men
I had watched her night & day besure & never
     slept agen
& when she turned to go O I'd caught her mantle then
& wooed her like a lover by my lonely side to stay
Aye knelt & worshipped on as love in beauty's bower
& clung upon her smiles as a bee upon a flower
And gave her heart my poesys all cropt in a sunny hour
As keepsakes & pledges to never fade away
But love never heeded to treasure up the may
So it went the common road with decay.

THE FLITTING

I've left mine own old home of homes
Green fields & every pleasant place
The summer like a stranger comes
I pause & hardly know her face
I miss the hazel's happy green
The bluebell's quiet hanging blooms
Where envy's sneer was never seen
Where staring malice never comes

I miss the heath its yellow furze
Molehills & rabbit tracts that lead
Through beesom ling & teazle burrs
That spread a wilderness indeed
The woodland oaks & all below
That their white powdered branches shield
The mossy paths – the very crow
Croaks music in my native field

I sit me in my corner chair
That seems to feel itself from home
& hear bird-music here & there
From 'awthorn hedge & orchard come
I hear but all is strange & new
– I sat on my old bench in June
The sailing puddocks shrill 'peelew'
O'er Royce Wood seemed a sweeter tune

I walk adown the narrow lane
The nightingale is singing now
But like to me she seems at loss
For Royce Wood & its shielding bough
I lean upon the window sill
The trees & summer happy seem
Green sunny green they shine – but still
My heart goes far away to dream

Of happiness & thoughts arise
With home-bred pictures many a one
Green lanes that shut out burning skies
& old crooked stiles to rest upon
Above them hangs the maple tree
Below grass swells a velvet hill
& little footpaths sweet to see
Goes seeking sweeter places still

With bye & bye a brook to cross
O'er which a little arch is thrown
No brook is here I feel the loss
From home & friends & all alone
– The stone pit with its shelvy sides
Seemed hanging rocks in my esteem
I miss the prospect far & wide
From Langley Bush & so I seem

Alone & in a stranger scene
Far far from spots my heart esteems
The closen with their ancient green
Heaths woods & pastures sunny streams
The 'awthorns here were hung with may
But still they seem in deader green
The sun e'en seems to lose its way
Nor knows the quarter it is in

I dwell on trifles like a child
I feel as ill becomes a man
& still my thoughts like weedlings wild
Grow up to blossom where they can
They turn to places known so long
& feel that joy was dwelling there
So home-fed pleasures fill the song
That has no present joys to heir

I read in books for happiness
But books are like the sea to joy
They change – as well give age the glass
To hunt its visage when a boy
For books they follow fashions new
& throw all old esteems away
In crowded streets flowers never grew
But many there hath died away

Some sing the pomps of chivalry
As legends of the ancient time
Where gold & pearls & mystery
Are shadows painted for sublime
But passions of sublimity
Belong to pain & simpler things
& David underneath a tree
Sought, when a shepherd, Salem's springs

Where moss did into cushions spring
Forming a seat of velvet hue
A small unnoticed trifling thing
To all but heaven's hailing dew
& David's crown hath passed away
Yet poesy breathes his shepherd skill
His palace lost – & to this day
The little moss is blooming still

Strange scenes mere shadows are to me
Vague unpersonifying things
I love with my old home to be
By quiet woods & gravel springs
Where little pebbles wear as smooth
As hermit's beads by gentle floods
Whose noises doth my spirits sooth
& warms them into singing moods

Here every tree is strange to me
All foreign things where e'er I go
There's none where boyhood made a swee
Or clambered up to rob a crow
No hollow tree or woodland bower
Well known when joy was beating high
Where beauty ran to shun a shower
& love took pains to keep her dry

& laid the shoaf upon the ground
To keep her from the dripping grass
& ran for stowks & set them round
Till scarce a drop of rain could pass
Through – where the maidens they reclined
& sung sweet ballads now forgot
Which brought sweet memories to the mind
But here no memory knows them not

There have I sat by many a tree
& leaned o'er many a rural stile
& conned my thoughts as joys to me
Nought heeding who might frown or smile
'Twas nature's beauty that inspired
My heart with raptures not its own
& she's a fame that never tires
How could I feel myself alone

No – pasture molehills used to lie
& talk to me of sunny days
& then the glad sheep resting by
All still in ruminating praise
Of summer & the pleasant place
& every weed & blossom too
Was looking upward in my face
With friendship welcome 'how do ye do'

All tenants of an ancient place
& heirs of noble heritage
Coeval they with Adam's race
& blest with more substantial age
For when the world first saw the sun
There little flowers beheld him too
& when his love for earth begun
They were the first his smiles to woo

There little lambtoe bunches springs
In red-tinged & begolden dye
For ever & like China kings
They come but never seem to die
There may-blooms with its little threads
Still comes upon the thorny bowers
& ne'er forgets those pinky heads
Like fairy pins amid the flowers

& still they bloom as on the day
They first crowned wilderness & rock
When Abel haply crowned with may
The firstlings of his little flock
& Eve might from the matted thorn
To deck her lone & lovely brow
Reach that same rose the heedless scorn
Misnames as the dog rosey now

Give me no high-flown fangled things
No haughty pomp in marching chime
Where muses play on golden strings
& splendour passes for sublime
Where cities stretch as far as fame
& fancy's straining eye can go
& piled until the sky for shame
Is stooping far away below

I love the verse that mild & bland
Breathes of green fields & open sky
I love the muse that in her hand
Bears wreaths of native poesy
Who walks nor skips the pasture brook
In scorn – but by the drinking horse
Leans o'er its little brig to look
How far the sallows lean across

& feels a rapture in her breast
Upon their root-fringed grains to mark
A hermit morehen's sedgy nest
Just like a naiad's summer bark
She counts the eggs she cannot reach
Admires the spot & loves it well
& yearns so nature's lessons teach
Amid such neighbourhoods to dwell

I love the muse who sits her down
Upon the molehill's little lap
Who feels no fear to stain her gown
& pauses by the hedgerow gap
Not with that affectation praise
Of song to sing & never see
A field flower grow in all her days
Or e'en a forest's aged tree

E'en here my simple feelings nurse
A love for every simple weed
& e'en this little 'shepherd's purse'
Grieves me to cut it up – Indeed
I feel at times a love & joy
For every weed & every thing
A feeling kindred from a boy
A feeling brought with every spring

& why – this 'shepherd's purse' that grows
In this strange spot – In days gone by
Grew in the little garden rows
Of my old home now left – And I
Feel what I never felt before
This weed an ancient neighbour here
& though I own the spot no more
Its every trifle makes it dear

The ivy at the parlour end
The woodbine at the garden gate
Are all & each affection's friend
That rendered parting desolate
But times will change & friends must part
& nature still can make amends
Their memory lingers round the heart
Like life whose essence is its friends

Time looks on pomp with careless moods
Or killing apathy's disdain
– So where old marble cities stood
Poor persecuted weeds remain
She feels a love for little things
That very few can feel beside
& still the grass eternal springs
Where castles stood & grandeur died

A WISH

Mine be a cot beside the hill;
A beehive's hum shall soothe my ear;
A willowy brook that turns a mill,
With many a fall shall linger near.

The swallow, oft, beneath my thatch
Shall twitter from her clay-built nest;
Oft shall the pilgrim lift the latch,
And share my meal, a welcome guest.

Around my ivied porch shall spring
Each fragrant flower that drinks the dew;
And Lucy, at her wheel, shall sing
In russet gown and apron blue.

The village church among the trees,
Where first our marriage vows were given,
With merry peals shall swell the breeze
And point with taper spire to heaven.

SAMUEL ROGERS   69

INFLUENCE OF
NATURAL OBJECTS

WRITTEN AT THE CLOSE OF SPRING

The garlands fade that spring so lately wove,
   Each simple flower which she had nurs'd in dew,
Anemones, that spangled every grove,
   The primrose wan, and harebell mildly blue.
No more shall violets linger in the dell,
   Or purple orchis variegate the plain,
Till Spring again shall call forth every bell
   And dress with hurried hands her wreaths again.
Ah, poor humanity! so frail, so fair,
   And the fond visions of thy early day,
Till tyrant passion and corrosive care
   Bid all thy fairy colours flee away!
Another May new birds and flowers shall bring;
Ah! why has happiness no second spring?

CHARLOTTE SMITH   73

TO A MOUNTAIN-DAISY
On turning one down, with the plough, in April 1786

Wee, modest, crimson-tipped flow'r,
Thou's met me in an evil hour;
For I maun crush amang the stoure
    Thy slender stem:
To spare thee now is past my pow'r,
    Thou bonie gem.

Alas! it's no thy neebor sweet,
The bonie lark, companion meet!
Bending thee 'mang the dewy weet!
    Wi's spreckl'd breast,
When upward-springing, blythe, to greet
    The purpling East.

Cauld blew the bitter-biting North
Upon thy early, humble birth;
Yet cheerfully thou glinted forth
    Amid the storm,
Scarce rear'd above the parent-earth
    Thy tender form.

The flaunting flow'rs our gardens yield,
High-shelt'ring woods and wa's maun shield,
But thou, beneath the random bield
    O' clod or stane,
Adorns the histie stibble-field,
      Unseen, alane.

There, in thy scanty mantle clad,
Thy snawie bosom sun-ward spread,
Thou lifts thy unassuming head
    In humble guise;
But now the share uptears thy bed,
    And low thou lies!

Such is the fate of artless maid,
Sweet flow'ret of the rural shade!
By love's simplicity betray'd
    And guileless trust,
Till she, like thee, all soil'd, is laid
    Low i' the dust.

Such is the fate of simple bard,
On life's rough ocean luckless starr'd!
Unskilful he to note the card
    Of prudent lore,
Till billows rage and gales blow hard,
    And whelm him o'er!

Such fate to suffering worth is giv'n,
Who long with wants and woes has striv'n,
By human pride or cunning driv'n
        To mis'ry's brink,
Till wrench'd of ev'ry stay but Heav'n,
        He, ruin'd, sink!

Ev'n thou who mourn'st the daisy's fate,
That fate is thine – no distant date;
Stern ruin's plough-share drives, elate,
        Full on thy bloom,
Till crush'd beneath the furrow's weight
        Shall be thy doom!

AH! SUN-FLOWER

Ah Sun-flower! weary of time,
Who countest the steps of the Sun:
Seeking after that sweet golden clime
Where the travellers journey is done.

Where the Youth pined away with desire,
And the pale Virgin shrouded in snow:
Arise from their graves and aspire,
Where my Sun-flower wishes to go.

WILLIAM BLAKE   77

SONNET, TO THE STRAWBERRY

The Strawberry blooms upon its lowly bed,
Plant of my native soil! – the Lime may fling
More potent fragrance on the zephyr's wing,
The milky Cocoa richer juices shed,
The white Guava lovelier blossoms spread –
But not like thee to fond remembrance bring
The vanish'd hours of life's enchanting spring;
Short calendar of joys for ever fled!
Thou bid'st the scenes of childhood rise to view,
The wild-wood path which fancy loves to trace;
Where veil'd in leaves, thy fruit of rosy hue
Lurk'd on its pliant stem with modest grace –
But ah! when thought would later years renew,
Alas, successive sorrows crowd the space!

GROWTH OF GENIUS FROM THE INFLUENCES OF NATURAL OBJECTS ON THE IMAGINATION IN BOYHOOD AND EARLY YOUTH

Wisdom and Spirit of the Universe!
Thou Soul, that art the Eternity of Thought!
And giv'st to forms and images a breath
And everlasting motion! not in vain,
By day or star-light, thus from my first dawn
Of Childhood didst Thou intertwine for me
The passions that build up our human Soul,
Nor with the mean and vulgar works of man
But with high objects, with enduring things,
With Life and Nature; purifying thus
The elements of feeling and of thought,
And sanctifying by such discipline
Both pain and fear, until we recognize
A grandeur in the beatings of the heart.
     Nor was this fellowship vouchsaf'd to me
With stinted kindness. In November days,
When vapours rolling down the valleys made
A lonely scene more lonesome; among woods
At noon, and 'mid the calm of summer nights,
When by the margin of the trembling lake,
Beneath the gloomy hills I homeward went
In solitude, such intercourse was mine;

'Twas mine among the fields both day and night,
And by the waters all the summer long.
   And in the frosty season when the sun
Was set, and, visible for many a mile,
The cottage windows through the twilight blazed,
I heeded not the summons:– happy time
It was indeed for all of us, to me
It was a time of rapture! clear and loud
The village clock toll'd six – I wheel'd about,
Proud and exulting, like an untir'd horse
That car'd not for his home.– All shod with steel
We hiss'd along the polish'd ice, in games
Confederate, imitative of the chase
And woodland pleasures, the resounding horn,
The pack loud bellowing, and the hunted hare.
So, through the darkness and the cold we flew,
And not a voice was idle: with the din
Meanwhile the precipices rang aloud,
The leafless trees and every icy crag
Tinkled like iron, while the distant hills
Into the tumult sent an alien sound
Of melancholy – not unnoticed, while the stars,
Eastward, were sparkling clear, and in the west
The orange sky of evening died away.
   Not seldom from the uproar I retired
Into a silent bay or sportively
Glanc'd sideway, leaving the tumultuous throng

To cut across the image of a star
That gleam'd upon the ice: and oftentimes,
When we had given our bodies to the wind,
And all the shadowy banks on either side
Came sweeping through the darkness spinning still
The rapid line of motion, then at once
Have I reclining back upon my heels
Stopp'd short: yet still the solitary cliffs
Wheel'd by me even as if the earth had roll'd
With visible motion her diurnal round!
Behind me did they stretch in solemn train,
Feebler and feebler, and I stood and watch'd
Till all was tranquil as a summer sea.

THIS LIME-TREE BOWER MY PRISON

In the June of 1797, some long-expected Friends [including Charles Lamb] paid a visit to the author's cottage; and on the morning of their arrival, he met with an accident, which disabled him from walking during the whole time of their stay. One evening, when they had left him for a few hours, he composed the following lines in the garden-bower.

Well, they are gone, and here must I remain,
This lime-tree bower my prison! I have lost
Such beauties and such feelings, as had been
Most sweet to my remembrance, even when age
Had dimmed mine eyes to blindness! They,
     meanwhile,
My friends, whom I may never meet again,
On springy heath, along the hill-top edge,
Wander in gladness, and wind down, perchance,
To that still roaring dell, of which I told;
The roaring dell, o'erwooded, narrow, deep,
And only speckled by the mid-day sun;
Where its slim trunk the ash from rock to rock
Flings arching like a bridge;– that branchless ash,
Unsunn'd and damp, whose few poor yellow leaves
Ne'er tremble in the gale, yet tremble still,
Fann'd by the waterfall! and there my friends
Behold the dark green file of long lank weeds,
That all at once (a most fantastic sight!)

Still nod and drip beneath the dripping edge
Of the blue clay-stone.

                    Now, my friends emerge
Beneath the wide wide heaven – and view again
The many-steepled tract magnificent
Of hilly fields and meadows, and the sea,
With some fair bark, perhaps, whose sails
      light up
The slip of smooth clear blue betwixt two isles
Of purple shadow! Yes! they wander on
In gladness all; but thou, methinks, most glad,
My gentle-hearted Charles! for thou hast pined
And hunger'd after Nature, many a year,
In the great city pent, winning thy way
With sad yet patient soul, through evil and pain
And strange calamity! Ah! slowly sink
Behind the western ridge, thou glorious sun!
Shine in the slant beams of the sinking orb,
Ye purple heath-flowers! richlier burn, ye clouds!
Live in the yellow light, ye distant groves!
And kindle, thou blue ocean! So my friend
Struck with deep joy may stand, as I have stood,
Silent with swimming sense; yea, gazing round
On the wild landscape, gaze till all doth seem
Less gross than bodily; a living thing
Which acts upon the mind – and with such hues

As clothe the Almighty Spirit, when he makes
Spirits perceive his presence.

                    A delight
Comes sudden on my heart, and I am glad
As I myself were there! Nor in this bower,
This little lime-tree bower, have I not mark'd
Much that has sooth'd me. Pale beneath the blaze
Hung the transparent foliage; and I watch'd
Some broad and sunny leaf, and lov'd to see
The shadow of the leaf and stem above
Dappling its sunshine! And that walnut-tree
Was richly ting'd, and a deep radiance lay
Full on the ancient ivy, which usurps
Those fronting elms, and now, with blackest mass
Makes their dark branches gleam a lighter hue
Through the late twilight: and though now the bat
Wheels silent by, and not a swallow twitters,
Yet still the solitary humble bee
Sings in the bean-flower! Henceforth I shall know
That Nature ne'er deserts the wise and pure;
No plot so narrow, be but Nature there,
No waste so vacant, but may well employ
Each faculty of sense, and keep the heart
Awake to Love and Beauty! and sometimes
'Tis well to be bereft of promis'd good,
That we may lift the soul, and contemplate

With lively joy the joys we cannot share.
My gentle-hearted Charles! when the last rook
Beat its straight path along the dusky air
Homewards, I blest it! deeming its black wing
(Now a dim speck, now vanishing in the light)
Had cross'd the mighty orb's dilated glory,
While thou stood'st gazing; or when all was still,
Flew creeking o'er thy head, and had a charm
For thee, my gentle-hearted Charles, to whom
No sound is dissonant which tells of Life.

MONT BLANC: LINES WRITTEN
IN THE VALE OF CHAMOUNI

I

The everlasting universe of things
Flows through the mind, and rolls its rapid waves,
Now dark – now glittering – now reflecting gloom –
Now lending splendour, where from secret springs
The source of human thought its tribute brings
Of waters,– with a sound but half its own,
Such as a feeble brook will oft assume,
In the wild woods, among the mountains lone,
Where waterfalls around it leap for ever,
Where woods and winds contend, and a vast river
Over its rocks ceaselessly bursts and raves.

II

Thus thou, Ravine of Arve – dark, deep Ravine –
Thou many-coloured, many-voiced vale,
Over whose pines, and crags, and caverns sail
Fast cloud shadows and sunbeams: awful scene,
Where Power in likeness of the Arve comes down
From the ice-gulfs that gird his secret throne,
Bursting through these dark mountains like the flame
Of lightning thro' the tempest;– thou dost lie,
Thy giant brood of pines around thee clinging,
Children of elder time, in whose devotion

The chainless winds still come and ever came
To drink their odours, and their mighty swinging
To hear – an old and solemn harmony;
Thine earthly rainbows stretched across the sweep
Of the ethereal waterfall, whose veil
Robes some unsculptured image; the strange sleep
Which when the voices of the desert fail
Wraps all in its own deep eternity;–
Thy caverns echoing to the Arve's commotion,
A loud, lone sound no other sound can tame;
Thou art pervaded with that ceaseless motion,
Thou art the path of that unresting sound –
Dizzy Ravine! and when I gaze on thee
I seem as in a trance sublime and strange
To muse on my own separate phantasy,
My own, my human mind, which passively
Now renders and receives fast influencings,
Holding an unremitting interchange
With the clear universe of things around;
One legion of wild thoughts, whose wandering wings
Now float above thy darkness, and now rest
Where that or thou art no unbidden guest,
In the still cave of the witch Poesy,
Seeking among the shadows that pass by
Ghosts of all things that are, some shade of thee,
Some phantom, some faint image; till the breast
From which they fled recalls them, thou art there!

III

Some say that gleams of a remoter world
Visit the soul in sleep,– that death is slumber,
And that its shapes the busy thoughts outnumber
Of those who wake and live.– I look on high;
Has some unknown omnipotence unfurled
The veil of life and death? or do I lie
In dream, and does the mightier world of sleep
Spread far around and inaccessibly
Its circles? For the very spirit fails,
Driven like a homeless cloud from steep to steep
That vanishes among the viewless gales!
Far, far above, piercing the infinite sky,
Mont Blanc appears,– still, snowy, and serene –
Its subject mountains their unearthly forms
Pile around it, ice and rock; broad vales between
Of frozen floods, unfathomable deeps,
Blue as the overhanging heaven, that spread
And wind among the accumulated steeps;
A desert peopled by the storms alone,
Save when the eagle brings some hunter's bone,
And the wolf tracks her there – how hideously
Its shapes are heaped around! rude, bare, and high,
Ghastly, and scarred, and riven.– Is this the scene
Where the old Earthquake-daemon taught her young
Ruin? Were these their toys? or did a sea
Of fire envelop once this silent snow?

None can reply – all seems eternal now.
The wilderness has a mysterious tongue
Which teaches awful doubt, or faith so mild,
So solemn, so serene, that man may be
But for such faith with nature reconciled;
Thou hast a voice, great Mountain, to repeal
Large codes of fraud and woe; not understood
By all, but which the wise, and great, and good
Interpret, or make felt, or deeply feel.

IV
The fields, the lakes, the forests, and the streams,
Ocean, and all the living things that dwell
Within the daedal earth; lightning, and rain,
Earthquake, and fiery flood, and hurricane,
The torpor of the year when feeble dreams
Visit the hidden buds, or dreamless sleep
Holds every future leaf and flower;– the bound
With which from that detested trance they leap;
The works and ways of man, their death and birth,
And that of him and all that his may be;
All things that move and breathe with toil and sound
Are born and die; revolve, subside, and swell.
Power dwells apart in its tranquillity,
Remote, serene, and inaccessible:
And *this*, the naked countenance of earth,
On which I gaze, even these primeval mountains

Teach the adverting mind. The glaciers creep
Like snakes that watch their prey, from their
    far fountains,
Slow rolling on; there, many a precipice
Frost and the Sun in scorn of mortal power
Have piled: dome, pyramid, and pinnacle,
A city of death, distinct with many a tower
And wall impregnable of beaming ice.
Yet not a city, but a flood of ruin
Is there, that from the boundaries of the sky
Rolls its perpetual stream; vast pines are strewing
Its destined path, or in the mangled soil
Branchless and shattered stand; the rocks,
    drawn down
From yon remotest waste, have overthrown
The limits of the dead and living world,
Never to be reclaimed. The dwelling-place
Of insects, beasts, and birds, becomes its spoil;
Their food and their retreat for ever gone,
So much of life and joy is lost. The race
Of man flies far in dread; his work and dwelling
Vanish, like smoke before the tempest's stream,
And their place is not known. Below, vast caves
Shine in the rushing torrent's restless gleam,
Which from those secret chasms in tumult welling
Meet in the vale, and one majestic River,
The breath and blood of distant lands, for ever

Rolls its loud waters to the ocean waves,
Breathes its swift vapours to the circling air.

V

Mont Blanc yet gleams on high:– the power is there,
The still and solemn power of many sights,
And many sounds, and much of life and death.
In the calm darkness of the moonless nights,
In the lone glare of day, the snows descend
Upon that Mountain; none beholds them there,
Nor when the flakes burn in the sinking sun,
Or the star-beams dart through them.–
            Winds contend
Silently there, and heap the snow with breath
Rapid and strong, but silently! Its home
The voiceless lightning in these solitudes
Keeps innocently, and like vapour broods
Over the snow. The secret strength of things
Which governs thought, and to the infinite dome
Of heaven is as a law, inhabits thee!
And what were thou, and earth, and stars, and sea,
If to the human mind's imaginings
Silence and solitude were vacancy?

FLOATING ISLAND

Harmonious Powers with Nature work
On sky, earth, river, lake, and sea;
Sunshine and cloud, whirlwind and breeze
All in one duteous task agree.

Once did I see a slip of earth
(By throbbing waves long undermined)
Loosed from its hold; how, no one knew,
But all might see it float, obedient to the wind;

Might see it, from the mossy shore
Dissevered, float upon the Lake,
Float with its crest of trees adorned
On which the warbling birds their pastime take.

Food, shelter, safety, there they find;
There berries ripen, flowerets bloom;
There insects live their lives, and die;
A peopled world it is; in size a tiny room.

And thus through many seasons' space
This little Island may survive;
But Nature, though we mark her not,
Will take away, may cease to give.

Perchance when you are wandering forth
Upon some vacant sunny day,
Without an object, hope, or fear,
Thither your eyes may turn – the Isle is passed away.

Buried beneath the glittering Lake,
Its place no longer to be found;
Yet the lost fragments shall remain,
To fertilize some other ground.

THE CATARACT OF LODORE
Described in rhymes for the nursery

'How does the water
Come down at Lodore?'
My little boy asked me
Thus, once on a time;
And moreover he tasked me
To tell him in rhyme.
Anon at the word,
There first came one daughter,
And then came another,
To second and third
The request of their brother,
And to hear how the water
Comes down at Lodore,
With its rush and its roar,
As many a time
They had seen it before.
So I told them in rhyme,
For of rhymes I had store;
And 'twas in my vocation
For their recreation
That so I should sing;
Because I was Laureate
To them and the King.

From its sources which well
In the tarn on the fell;
From its fountains
In the mountains,
Its rills and its gills;
Through moss and through brake,
It runs and it creeps
For awhile, till it sleeps
In its own little lake.
And thence at departing,
Awakening and starting,
It runs through the reeds
And away it proceeds,
Through meadow and glade,
In sun and in shade,
And through the wood-shelter,
Among crags in its flurry,
Helter-skelter,
Hurry-scurry.
Here it comes sparkling,
And there it lies darkling;
Now smoking and frothing
Its tumult and wrath in,
Till in this rapid race
On which it is bent,
It reaches the place
Of its steep descent.

The cataract strong
Then plunges along,
Striking and raging
As if a war waging
Its caverns and rocks among:
Rising and leaping,
Sinking and creeping,
Swelling and sweeping,
Showering and springing,
Flying and flinging,
Writhing and ringing,
Eddying and whisking,
Spouting and frisking,
Turning and twisting,
Around and around
With endless rebound;
Smiting and fighting,
A sight to delight in;
Confounding, astounding,
Dizzying and deafening the ear with its sound.

Collecting, projecting,
Receding and speeding,
And shocking and rocking,
And darting and parting,
And threading and spreading,
And whizzing and hissing,

And dripping and skipping,
And hitting and splitting,
And shining and twining,
And rattling and battling,
And shaking and quaking,
And pouring and roaring,
And waving and raving,
And tossing and crossing,
And flowing and going,
And running and stunning,
And foaming and roaming,
And dinning and spinning,
And dropping and hopping,
And working and jerking,
And guggling and struggling,
And heaving and cleaving,
And moaning and groaning;

And glittering and frittering,
And gathering and feathering,
And whitening and brightening,
And quivering and shivering,
And hurrying and skurrying,
And thundering and floundering;

Dividing and gliding and sliding,
And falling and brawling and sprawling,

And driving and riving and striving,
And sprinkling and twinkling and wrinkling,
And sounding and bounding and rounding,
And bubbling and troubling and doubling,
And grumbling and rumbling and tumbling,
And clattering and battering and shattering;

Retreating and beating and meeting and sheeting,
Delaying and straying and playing and spraying,
Advancing and prancing and glancing and dancing,
Recoiling, turmoiling and toiling and boiling,
And gleaming and streaming and steaming
and beaming,
And rushing and flushing and brushing and gushing,
And flapping and rapping and clapping and slapping,
And curling and whirling and purling and twirling,
And thumping and plumping and bumping
and jumping,
And dashing and flashing and splashing and clashing;
And so never ending, but always descending,
Sounds and motions for ever and ever are blending
All at once and all o'er, with a mighty uproar,
And this way the water comes down at Lodore.

AIREY FORCE

Aye, underneath yon shadowy side,
  I could be fain to fix my home;
Where dashes down the torrent's pride,
  In sparkling wave, and silver foam.

No other sound is waking there,
  But that perpetual voice, which seems
Like spirit-music on the air,
  An echo from the world of dreams.

They were more wise in other days;
  Then turned the hermit to his cell,
And left a world where all betrays,
  Apart with his own thoughts to dwell.

Content to curb the heart, to be
  Indifferent, quiet, mournful, cold
With hopes turned into memory,
  With feelings that had lost their hold.

Far better this, than such vain life
  As is in crowded cities known;
Where care, repining, grief, and strife,
  Make every passing hour their own.

There, by yon torrent's rushing wave,
  I'd pass what yet of time remain'd;
And feel the quiet of the grave
  Long ere that grave itself were gain'd.

from BEACHY HEAD

On thy stupendous summit, rock sublime!
That o'er the channel rear'd, half way at sea
The mariner at early morning hails,
I would recline; while Fancy should go forth,
And represent the strange and awful hour
Of vast concussion; when the Omnipotent
Stretch'd forth his arm, and rent the solid hills,
Bidding the impetuous main flood rush between
The rifted shores, and from the continent
Eternally divided this green isle.
Imperial lord of the high southern coast!
From thy projecting head-land I would mark
Far in the east the shades of night disperse,
Melting and thinned, as from the dark blue wave
Emerging, brilliant rays of arrowy light
Dart from the horizon; when the glorious sun
Just lifts above it his resplendent orb.
Advances now, with feathery silver touched,
The rippling tide of flood; glisten the sands,
While, inmates of the chalky clefts that scar
Thy sides precipitous, with shrill harsh cry,
Their white wings glancing in the level beam,
The terns, and gulls, and tarrocks, seek their food,
And thy rough hollows echo to the voice
Of the gray choughs, and ever restless daws,

With clamour, not unlike the chiding hounds,
While the lone shepherd, and his baying dog,
Drive to thy turfy crest his bleating flock.

The high meridian of the day is past,
And Ocean now, reflecting the calm Heaven,
Is of cerulean hue; and murmurs low
The tide of ebb, upon the level sands.
The sloop, her angular canvas shifting still,
Catches the light and variable airs
That but a little crisp the summer sea,
Dimpling its tranquil surface.

* * *

The fishermen, who at set seasons pass
Many a league off at sea their toiling night,
Now hail their comrades, from their daily task
Returning; and make ready for their own,
With the night tide commencing:– The night tide
Bears a dark vessel on, whose hull and sails
Mark her a coaster from the north. Her keel
Now ploughs the sand; and sidelong now she leans,
While with loud clamours her athletic crew
Unload her; and resounds the busy hum
Along the wave-worn rocks. Yet more remote,
Where the rough cliff hangs beetling o'er its base,

All breathes repose; the water's rippling sound
Scarce heard; but now and then the sea-snipe's cry
Just tells that something living is abroad;
And sometimes crossing on the moonbright line
Glimmers the skiff, faintly discern'd awhile,
Then lost in shadow.

* * *

An early worshipper at Nature's shrine,
I loved her rudest scenes – warrens, and heaths,
And yellow commons, and birch-shaded hollows,
And hedge rows, bordering unfrequented lanes
Bowered with wild roses, and the clasping woodbine
Where purple tassels of the tangling vetch
With bittersweet, and bryony inweave,
And the dew fills the silver bindweed's cups –
I loved to trace the brooks whose humid banks
Nourish the harebell, and the freckled pagil;
And stroll among o'ershadowing woods of beech,
Lending in summer, from the heats of noon
A whispering shade; while haply there reclines
Some pensive lover of uncultur'd flowers,
Who, from the tumps with bright green mosses clad,
Plucks the wood sorrel, with its light thin leaves,
Heart-shaped, and triply folded; and its root
Creeping like beaded coral; or who there

Gathers, the copse's pride, anemones,
With rays like golden studs on ivory laid
Most delicate: but touched with purple clouds,
Fit crowns for April's fair but changeful brow.

Ah! hills so early loved! In fancy still
I breathe your pure keen air; and still behold
Those widely spreading views, mocking alike
The Poet and the Painter's utmost art.
And still, observing objects more minute,
Wondering remark the strange and foreign forms
Of sea-shells; with the pale calcareous soil
Mingled, and seeming of resembling substance.
Tho' surely the blue Ocean (from the heights
Where the downs westward trend, but dimly seen)
Here never roll'd its surge. Does Nature then
Mimic, in wanton mood, fantastic shapes
Of bivalves, and inwreathed volutes, that cling
To the dark sea-rock of the wat'ry world?
Or did this range of chalky mountains, once
Form a vast basin, where the Ocean waves
Swell'd fathomless?

THE PETTICHAP'S NEST

Well, in my many walks I rarely found
A place less likely for a bird to form
Its nest close by the rut-gulled wagon road
And on the almost bare foot-trodden ground
With scarce a clump of grass to keep it warm
And not a thistle spreads its spears abroad
Or prickly bush to shield it from harm's way
And yet so snugly made that none may spy
It out, save accident – and you and I
Had surely passed it on our walk today
Had chance not led us by it – nay e'en now
Had not the old bird heard us trampling by
And fluttered out – we had not seen it lie
Brown as the roadway side – small bits of hay
Plucked from the old propped-haystack's pleachy brow
And withered leaves make up its outward walls
That from the snub-oak dotterel yearly falls
And in the old hedge bottom rot away
Built like an oven with a little hole
Hard to discover – that snug entrance wins
Scarcely admitting e'en two fingers in
And lined with feathers warm as silken stole
And soft as seats of down for painless ease
And full of eggs scarce bigger e'en than peas
Here's one most delicate with spots as small

As dust – and of a faint and pinky red
– We'll let them be and safety guard them well
For fear's rude paths around are thickly spread
And they are left to many dangers' ways
When green grasshopper's jump might break
    the shells
While lowing oxen pass them morn and night
And restless sheep around them hourly stray
And no grass springs but hungry horses bite
That trample past them twenty times a day
Yet like a miracle in safety's lap
They still abide unhurt and out of sight
– Stop, here's the bird. That woodman at the gap
Hath put it from the hedge – 'tis olive green
Well I declare it is the pettichap
Not bigger than the wren and seldom seen
I've often found their nests in chance's way
When I in pathless woods did idly roam
But never did I dream until today
A spot like this would be her chosen home

PEWIT'S NEST

Across the fallow clods at early morn
I took a random track where scant & spare
The grass & nibbled leaves all closely shorn
Leaves a burnt flat all bleaching brown & bare
Where hungry sheep in freedom range forlorn
& neath the leaning willow & odd thorn
& molehill large that vagrant shade supplies
They batter round to shun the teasing flies
Trampling smooth places hard as cottage floors
Where the time-killing lonely shepherd boys
Whose summer homes are ever out of doors
Their chock-holes form & chalk their marble ring
& make their clay taws at the bubbling spring
& in their wrangling sport & gambling joys
They strain their clocklike shadows – when it cloys
To guess the hour that slowly runs away
& shorten sultry turmoil with their play
Here did I roam while veering overhead
The pewit whirred in many whewing rings
& 'chewsit' screamed & clapped her flapping wings
To hunt her nest my rambling steps was led
O'er the broad baulk beset with little hills
By moles long formed & pismires tenanted
As likely spots – but still I searched in vain
When all at once the noisy birds were still

& on the lands a furrowed ridge between
Chance found four eggs of dingy dirty green
Deep blotched with plashy spots of chocolate stain
Their small ends inward turned as ever found
As though some curious hand had laid them round
Yet lying on the ground with nought at all
Of soft grass withered twitch & bleached weed
To keep them from the rain storms' frequent fall
& here she broods on her unsavory bed
When bye & bye with little care & heed
Her young with each a shell upon its head
Run after their wild parents' restless cry
& from their own fears tiny shadows run
Neath clods & stones to cringe & snugly lie
Hid from all sight but the all-seeing sun
Till never ceasing danger seemeth by

THE SKYLARK

Above the russet clods, the corn is seen
Sprouting its spiry points of tender green,
Where squats the hare, to terrors wide awake,
Like some brown clod the harrows failed to break.
Opening their golden caskets to the sun,
The buttercups make schoolboys eager run,
To see who shall be first to pluck the prize –
Up from their hurry see the skylark flies,
And o'er her half-formed nest, with happy wings
Winnows the air, till in the cloud she sings,
Then hangs a dust spot in the sunny skies,
And drops, and drops, till in her nest she lies,
Which they unheeded passed – not dreaming then
That birds, which flew so high, would drop again
To nests upon the ground, which any thing
May come at to destroy. Had they the wing
Like such a bird, themselves would be too proud,
And build on nothing but a passing cloud!
As free from danger, as the heavens are free
From pain and toil, there would they build, and be,
And sail about the world to scenes unheard
Of and unseen,– O were they but a bird!
So think they, while they listen to its song,
And smile, and fancy, and so pass along;

While its low nest, moist with the dews of morn,
Lies safely, with the leveret, in the corn.

TO A SKYLARK

Hail to thee, blithe spirit!
   Bird thou never wert,
That from heaven, or near it,
   Pourest thy full heart
In profuse strains of unpremeditated art.

Higher still and higher,
   From the earth thou springest
Like a cloud of fire;
   The blue deep thou wingest,
And singing still dost soar, and soaring ever singest.

In the golden lightning
   Of the sunken sun,
O'er which clouds are brightning,
   Thou dost float and run;
Like an unbodied joy whose race is just begun.

The pale purple even
   Melts around thy flight;
Like a star of heaven,
   In the broad day-light
Thou art unseen, but yet I hear thy shrill delight,

Keen as are the arrows
    Of that silver sphere,
Whose intense lamp narrows
    In the white dawn clear,
Until we hardly see, we feel that it is there.

All the earth and air
    With thy voice is loud,
As, when night is bare,
    From one lonely cloud
The moon rains out her beams, and heaven is
    overflowed.

What thou art we know not;
    What is most like thee?
From rainbow clouds there flow not
    Drops so bright to see
As from thy presence showers a rain of melody.

Like a poet hidden
    In the light of thought,
Singing hymns unbidden,
    Till the world is wrought
To sympathy with hopes and fears it heeded not:

Like a high-born maiden
  In a palace-tower,
Soothing her love-laden
  Soul in secret hour
With music sweet as love, which overflows her bower:

Like a glow-worm golden
  In a dell of dew,
Scattering unbeholden
  Its aërial hue
Among the flowers and grass, which screen it from
  the view:

Like a rose embowered
  In its own green leaves,
By warm winds deflowered,
  Till the scent it gives
Makes faint with too much sweet those heavy-winged
  thieves:

Sound of vernal showers
  On the twinkling grass,
Rain-awakened flowers,
  All that ever was
Joyous, and clear, and fresh, thy music doth surpass.

Teach us, sprite or bird,
    What sweet thoughts are thine:
I have never heard
    Praise of love or wine
That panted forth a flood of rapture so divine.

Chorus hymeneal,
    Or triumphal chant,
Matched with thine would be all
    But an empty vaunt –
A thing wherein we feel there is some hidden want.

What objects are the fountains
    Of thy happy strain?
What fields, or waves, or mountains?
    What shapes of sky or plain?
What love of thine own kind? what ignorance of pain?

With thy clear keen joyance
    Languor cannot be:
Shadow of annoyance
    Never came near thee:
Thou lovest; but ne'er knew love's sad satiety.

Waking or asleep,
    Thou of death must deem
Things more true and deep
    Than we mortals dream,
Or how could thy notes flow in such a crystal stream?

We look before and after,
    And pine for what is not:
Our sincerest laughter
    With some pain is fraught;
Our sweetest songs are those that tell of saddest
    thought.

Yet if we could scorn
    Hate, and pride, and fear;
If we were things born
    Not to shed a tear,
I know not how thy joy we ever should come near.

Better than all measures
    Of delightful sound,
Better than all treasures
    That in books are found,
Thy skill to poet were, thou scorner of the ground!

Teach me half the gladness
    That thy brain must know,
Such harmonious madness
    From my lips would flow,
The world should listen then, as I am listening now.

TO THE GRASSHOPPER AND
THE CRICKET

Green little vaulter in the sunny grass,
　　Catching your heart up at the feel of June,
　　Sole voice that's heard amidst the lazy noon,
When even the bees lag at the summoning brass
And you, warm little housekeeper, who class
　　With those who think the candles come too soon,
　　Loving the fire, and with your tricksome tune
Nick the glad silent moments as they pass;

Oh sweet and tiny cousins, that belong,
　　One to the fields, the other to the hearth,
Both have your sunshine; both, though small,
　　　　are strong
　　At your clear hearts; and both seem given to earth
To ring in thoughtful ears this natural song –
　　In doors and out, summer and winter, Mirth.

LEIGH HUNT　　　　　　　　　　　　　　　117

ON THE GRASSHOPPER AND CRICKET

The poetry of earth is never dead:
  When all the birds are faint with the hot sun,
  And hide in cooling trees, a voice will run
From hedge to hedge about the new-mown mead;
That is the Grasshopper's – he takes the lead
  In summer luxury,– he has never done
  With his delights; for when tired out with fun
He rests at ease beneath some pleasant weed.
The poetry of earth is ceasing never:
  On a lone winter evening, when the frost
    Has wrought a silence, from the stove there shrills
The Cricket's song, in warmth increasing ever,
  And seems to one in drowsiness half lost,
    The Grasshopper's among some grassy hills.

TO AUTUMN

Season of mists and mellow fruitfulness,
  Close bosom-friend of the maturing sun;
Conspiring with him how to load and bless
  With fruit the vines that round the thatch-eves run;
To bend with apples the moss'd cottage-trees,
  And fill all fruit with ripeness to the core;
    To swell the gourd, and plump the hazel shells
With a sweet kernel; to set budding more,
  And still more, later flowers for the bees,
  Until they think warm days will never cease,
    For summer has o'er-brimm'd their clammy cells.

Who hath not seen thee oft amid thy store?
  Sometimes whoever seeks abroad may find
Thee sitting careless on a granary floor,
  Thy hair soft-lifted by the winnowing wind;
Or on a half-reap'd furrow sound asleep,
  Drows'd with the fume of poppies, while thy hook
    Spares the next swath and all its twined flowers:
And sometimes like a gleaner thou dost keep
  Steady thy laden head across a brook;
  Or by a cyder-press, with patient look,
    Thou watchest the last oozings hours by hours.

Where are the songs of spring? Ay, where are they?
Think not of them, thou hast thy music too –
While barred clouds bloom the soft-dying day,
And touch the stubble-plains with rosy hue;
Then in a wailful choir the small gnats mourn
Among the river sallows, borne aloft
Or sinking as the light wind lives or dies;
And full-grown lambs loud bleat from hilly bourn;
Hedge-crickets sing; and now with treble soft
The red-breast whistles from a garden-croft;
And gathering swallows twitter in the skies.

from THE SHEPHERD'S CALENDAR:
OCTOBER

Like to a painted map the landscape lies
And wild above shine the cloud-thronged skies
The flying clouds urged on in swiftest pace
Like living things as if they runned a race
The winds that o'er each coming tempest broods
Waking like spirits in their startling moods
Fluttering the sear leaves on the black'ning lea
That litters under every fading tree
And pausing oft as falls the patting rain
Then gathering strength and twirling them again
Till drops the sudden calm – the hurried mill
Is stopped at once and every noise is still
The startled stock-dove hurried whizzing by
As the still hawk hangs o'er him in the sky
Crows from the oak trees quawking as they spring
Dashing the acorns down wi' beating wing
Waking the woodland's sleep in noises low
Patting the crimped brake's withering brown below
The starnel crowds that dim the muddy light
And puddock circling round its lazy flight
Round the wild sweeing wood in motion slow
Before it perches on the oaks below
And huge black beetles revelling alone
In the dull evening with their heavy drone

Buzzing from barn door straw and hovel sides
Where foddered cattle from the night abides
These pictures linger thro' the short'ning day
And cheer the lone bard's melancholy way
Till surly Winter comes with biting breath
And strips the woods and numbs the scene with death
Then all is still o'er wood and field and plain
As nought had been and nought would be again

ODE TO THE WEST WIND

I

O wild West Wind, thou breath of Autumn's being,
Thou, from whose unseen presence the leaves dead
Are driven, like ghosts from an enchanter fleeing,

Yellow, and black, and pale, and hectic red,
Pestilence-stricken multitudes: O thou,
Who chariotest to their dark wintry bed

The winged seeds, where they lie cold and low,
Each like a corpse within its grave, until
Thine azure sister of the Spring shall blow

Her clarion o'er the dreaming earth, and fill
(Driving sweet buds like flocks to feed in air)
With living hues and odours plain and hill:

Wild Spirit, which art moving everywhere;
Destroyer and preserver; hear, oh hear!

II

Thou on whose stream, 'mid the steep sky's
        commotion,
Loose clouds like earth's decaying leaves are shed,
Shook from the tangled boughs of Heaven and Ocean,

Angels of rain and lightning: there are spread
On the blue surface of thine airy surge,
Like the bright hair uplifted from the head

Of some fierce Maenad, even from the dim verge
Of the horizon to the zenith's height,
The locks of the approaching storm. Thou dirge

Of the dying year, to which this closing night
Will be the dome of a vast sepulchre,
Vaulted with all thy congregated might

Of vapours, from whose solid atmosphere
Black rain, and fire, and hail will burst: Oh hear!

III

Thou who didst waken from his summer dreams
The blue Mediterranean, where he lay,
Lull'd by the coil of his crystalline streams,

Beside a pumice isle in Baiae's bay,
And saw in sleep old palaces and towers
Quivering within the wave's intenser day,

All overgrown with azure moss and flowers
So sweet, the sense faints picturing them! Thou
For whose path the Atlantic's level powers

Cleave themselves into chasms, while far below
The sea-blooms and the oozy woods which wear
The sapless foliage of the ocean, know

Thy voice, and suddenly grow grey with fear,
And tremble and despoil themselves: Oh hear!

IV

If I were a dead leaf thou mightest bear;
If I were a swift cloud to fly with thee;
A wave to pant beneath thy power, and share

The impulse of thy strength, only less free
Than thou, O uncontrollable! If even
I were as in my boyhood, and could be

The comrade of thy wanderings over Heaven,
As then, when to outstrip thy skyey speed
Scarce seemed a vision; I would ne'er have striven

As thus with thee in prayer in my sore need.
Oh! lift me as a wave, a leaf, a cloud!
I fall upon the thorns of life! I bleed!

A heavy weight of hours has chained and bowed
One too like thee: tameless, and swift, and proud.

V

Make me thy lyre, even as the forest is:
What if my leaves are falling like its own!
The tumult of thy mighty harmonies

Will take from both a deep autumnal tone,
Sweet though in sadness. Be thou, spirit fierce,
My spirit! Be thou me, impetuous one!

Drive my dead thoughts over the universe
Like withered leaves to quicken a new birth;
And, by the incantation of this verse,

Scatter, as from an unextinguished hearth
Ashes and sparks, my words among mankind!
Be through my lips to unawakened earth

The trumpet of a prophecy! O wind,
If Winter comes, can Spring be far behind?

EMMONSAILS HEATH IN WINTER

I love to see the old heath's withered brake
Mingle its crimpled leaves with furze and ling
While the old heron from the lonely lake
Starts slow and flaps its melancholy wing
And oddling crow in idle motion swing
On the half-rotten ash-tree's topmost twig
Beside whose trunk the gypsy makes his bed
Up flies the bouncing woodcock from the brig
Where a black quagmire quakes beneath the tread
The fieldfare chatters in the whistling thorn
And for the haw round fields and closen rove
And coy bumbarrels twenty in a drove
Flit down the hedgerows in the frozen plain
And hang on little twigs and start again

JOHN CLARE   127

SUDDEN SHOWER

Black grows the southern sky, betokening rain,
　And humming hive-bees homeward hurry by:
They feel the change; so let us shun the grain,
　And take the broad road while our feet are dry.
Aye there, some drops fell moistening on my face,
　And pattering on my hat – 'tis coming nigh! –
Let's look about, and find a sheltering place.
　The little things around us fear the sky,
And hasten through the grass to shun the shower.
　Here stoops an ash-tree – hark! the wind gets high,
But never mind; this ivy, for an hour,
　Rain as it may, will keep us drily here:
That little wren knows well his sheltering bower,
　Nor leaves his covert, though we come so near.

from CHILDE HAROLD'S PILGRIMAGE

Lake Leman woos me with its crystal face,
The mirror where the stars and mountains view
The stillness of their aspect in each trace
Its clear depth yields of their far height and hue:
There is too much of man here, to look through
With a fit mind the might which I behold;
But soon in me shall Loneliness renew
Thoughts hid, but not less cherish'd than of old,
Ere mingling with the herd had penn'd me in their fold.

To fly from, need not be to hate, mankind:
All are not fit with them to stir and toil,
Nor is it discontent to keep the mind
Deep in its fountain, lest it overboil
In one hot throng, where we become the spoil
Of our infection, till too late and long
We may deplore and struggle with the coil,
In wretched interchange of wrong for wrong
Midst a contentious world, striving where none
    are strong.

There, in a moment, we may plunge our years
In fatal penitence, and in the blight
Of our own soul, turn all our blood to tears,
And colour things to come with hues of Night;
The race of life becomes a hopeless flight
To those that walk in darkness: on the sea,
The boldest steer but where their ports invite;
But there are wanderers o'er Eternity
Whose bark drives on and on, and anchor'd ne'er
    shall be.

Is it not better, then, to be alone,
And love Earth only for its earthly sake?
By the blue rushing of the arrowy Rhone,
Or the pure bosom of its nursing lake,
Which feeds it as a mother who doth make
A fair but froward infant her own care,
Kissing its cries away as these awake;—
Is it not better thus our lives to wear,
Than join the crushing crowd, doom'd to inflict
    or bear?

I live not in myself, but I become
Portion of that around me; and to me,
High mountains are a feeling, but the hum
Of human cities torture: I can see
Nothing to loathe in nature, save to be
A link reluctant in a fleshly chain,
Class'd among creatures, when the soul can flee,
And with the sky, the peak, the heaving plain
Of ocean, or the stars, mingle, and not in vain.

And thus I am absorb'd, and this is life;
I look upon the peopled desert past,
As on a place of agony and strife,
Where, for some sin, to sorrow I was cast,
To act and suffer, but remount at last
With a fresh pinion; which I felt to spring,
Though young, yet waxing vigorous as the blast
Which it would cope with, on delighted wing,
Spurning the clay-cold bonds which round our
        being cling.

And when, at length, the mind shall be all free
From what it hates in this degraded form,
Reft of its carnal life, save what shall be
Existent happier in the fly and worm,–
When elements to elements conform,
And dust is as it should be, shall I not
Feel all I see, less dazzling, but more warm?
The bodiless thought? the Spirit of each spot?
Of which, even now, I share at times the immortal lot?

Are not the mountains, waves, and skies a part
Of me and of my soul, as I of them?
Is not the love of these deep in my heart
With a pure passion? should I not contemn
All objects, if compared with these? and stem
A tide of suffering, rather than forego
Such feelings for the hard and worldly phlegm
Of those whose eyes are only turn'd below,
Gazing upon the ground, with thoughts which dare
    not glow?

THE ROCK OF CADER IDRIS

It is an old tradition of the Welsh bards, that on the summit of the mountain Cader Idris is an excavation resembling a couch; and that whoever should pass a night in that hollow, would be found in the morning either dead, in a state of frenzy, or endowed with the highest poetical inspiration.

I lay on that rock where the storms have their dwelling,
   The birthplace of phantoms, the home of the cloud;
Around it for ever deep music is swelling,
   The voice of the mountain-wind, solemn and loud.
'Twas a midnight of shadows all fitfully streaming,
   Of wild waves and breezes, that mingled their moan;
Of dim shrouded stars, as from gulfs faintly gleaming;
   And I met the dread gloom of its grandeur alone.

I lay there in silence – a spirit came o'er me;
   Man's tongue hath no language to speak what I saw:
Things glorious, unearthly, pass'd floating before me,
   And my heart almost fainted with rapture and awe.
I view'd the dread beings around us that hover,
   Though veil'd by the mists of mortality's breath;
And I call'd upon darkness the vision to cover,
   For a strife was within me of madness and death.

I saw them – the powers of the wind and the ocean,
  The rush of whose pinion bears onward the storms;
Like the sweep of the white-rolling wave was their
      motion,
    I *felt* their dim presence,– but knew not their forms!
I saw them – the mighty of ages departed –
  The dead were around me that night on the hill:
From their eyes, as they pass'd, a cold radiance
      they darted,–
    There was light on my soul, but my heart's blood
        was chill.

I saw what man looks on, and dies – but my spirit
  Was strong, and triumphantly lived through
      that hour;
And, as from the grave, I awoke to inherit
  A flame all immortal, a voice, and a power!
Day burst on that rock with the purple cloud crested,
  And high Cader Idris rejoiced in the sun;–
But O! what new glory all nature invested,
  When the sense which gives soul to her beauty
      was won!

ON THE SEA

It keeps eternal whisperings around
Desolate shores, and with its mighty swell
Gluts twice ten thousand caverns, till the spell
Of Hecate leaves them their old shadowy sound.
Often 'tis in such gentle temper found,
That scarcely will the very smallest shell
Be moved for days from where it sometime fell.
When last the winds of heaven were unbound.
O ye who have your eyeballs vexed and tired,
Feast them upon the wideness of the sea;
O ye whose ears are dinned with uproar rude,
Or fed too much with cloying melody,
Sit ye near some old cavern's mouth and brood
Until ye start, as if the sea nymphs quired!

THE TYGER

Tyger Tyger: burning bright,
In the forests of the night:
What immortal hand or eye,
Could frame thy fearful symmetry?

In what distant deeps or skies.
Burnt the fire of thine eyes?
On what wings dare he aspire?
What the hand, dare seize the fire?

And what shoulder, & what art,
Could twist the sinews of thy heart?
And when thy heart began to beat,
What dread hand? & what dread feet?

What the hammer? what the chain,
In what furnace was thy brain?
What the anvil? what dread grasp,
Dare its deadly terrors clasp!

When the stars threw down their spears
And water'd heaven with their tears:
Did he smile his work to see?
Did he who made the Lamb make thee?

Tyger Tyger burning bright,
In the forests of the night:
What immortal hand or eye,
Dare frame thy fearful symmetry?

SOCIETY AND
POLITICS

LONDON'S SUMMER MORNING

Who has not wak'd to list the busy sounds
Of summer's morning, in the sultry smoke
Of noisy London? On the pavement hot
The sooty chimney-boy, with dingy face
And tattered covering, shrilly bawls his trade,
Rousing the sleepy housemaid. At the door
The milk-pail rattles, and the tinkling bell
Proclaims the dustman's office; while the street
Is lost in clouds impervious. Now begins
The din of hackney-coaches, wagons, carts;
While tinmen's shops, and noisy trunk-makers,
Knife-grinders, coopers, squeaking cork-cutters,
Fruit-barrows, and the hunger-giving cries
Of vegetable-vendors, fill the air.
Now every shop displays its varied trade,
And the fresh-sprinkled pavement cools the feet
Of early walkers. At the private door
The ruddy housemaid twirls the busy mop,
Annoying the smart 'prentice, or neat girl,
Tripping with band-box lightly. Now the sun
Darts burning splendour on the glitt'ring pane,
Save where the canvas awning throws a shade
On the gay merchandise. Now, spruce and trim,
In shops (where beauty smiles with industry)
Sits the smart damsel; while the passenger

Peeps thro' the window, watching ev'ry charm.
Now pastry dainties catch the eye minute
Of humming insects, while the limy snare
Waits to enthrall them. Now the lamp-lighter
Mounts the tall ladder, nimbly vent'rous,
To trim the half-fill'd lamps, while at his feet
The pot-boy yells discordant! All along
The sultry pavement, the old-clothes-man cries
In tone monotonous, and sidelong views
The area for his traffic: now the bag
Is slyly open'd, and the half-worn suit
(Sometimes the pilfer'd treasure of the base
Domestic spoiler), for one half its worth,
Sinks in the green abyss. The porter now
Bears his huge load along the burning way;
And the poor poet wakes from busy dreams,
To paint the summer morning.

COMPOSED UPON
WESTMINSTER BRIDGE
Sept. 3, 1803

Earth has not any thing to show more fair:
Dull would he be of soul who could pass by
A sight so touching in its majesty:
This City now doth like a garment wear
The beauty of the morning; silent, bare,
Ships, towers, domes, theatres, and temples lie
Open unto the fields, and to the sky;
All bright and glittering in the smokeless air.
Never did sun more beautifully steep
In his first splendour valley, rock, or hill;
Ne'er saw I, never felt, a calm so deep!
The river glideth at his own sweet will:
Dear God! the very houses seem asleep;
And all that mighty heart is lying still!

WILLIAM WORDSWORTH   143

LONDON

I wander thro' each charter'd street
Near where the charter'd Thames does flow
And mark in every face I meet
Marks of weakness marks of woe.

In every cry of every Man
In every Infant's cry of fear
In every voice: in every ban,
The mind-forg'd manacles I hear

How the Chimney-sweeper's cry
Every black'ning Church appalls,
And the hapless Soldier's sigh
Runs in blood down Palace walls

But most thro' midnight streets I hear
How the youthful Harlot's curse
Blasts the new-born Infant's tear
And blights with plagues the Marriage hearse.

THE GARDEN OF LOVE

I went to the Garden of Love,
And saw what I never had seen:
A Chapel was built in the midst,
Where I used to play on the green.

And the gates of this Chapel were shut,
And 'Thou shalt not' writ over the door;
So I turn'd to the Garden of Love,
That so many sweet flowers bore.

And I saw it was filled with graves,
And tomb-stones where flowers should be:
And Priests in black gowns, were walking
    their rounds,
And binding with briars, my joys & desires.

WILLIAM BLAKE

from SLAVERY: A POEM

Whene'er to Afric's shores I turn my eyes,
Horrors of deepest, deadliest guilt arise;
I see, by more than Fancy's mirror shewn,
The burning village, and the blazing town:
See the dire victim torn from social life,
The shrieking babe, the agonizing wife!
She, wretch forlorn! is dragg'd by hostile hands,
To distant tyrants sold, in distant lands!
Transmitted miseries, and successive chains,
The sole sad heritage her child obtains!
Ev'n this last wretched boon their foes deny,
To weep together, or together die.
By felon hands, by one relentless stroke,
See the fond links of feeling Nature broke!
The fibres twisting round a parent's heart,
Torn from their grasp, and bleeding as they part.

POEMS ON THE SLAVE TRADE: SONNET VI

High in the air expos'd the Slave is hung
To all the birds of Heaven, their living food!
He groans not, tho' awaked by that fierce Sun
New torturers live to drink their parent blood!
He groans not, tho' the gorging Vulture tear
The quivering fibre! hither gaze O ye
Who tore this Man from Peace and Liberty!
Gaze hither ye who weigh with scrupulous care
The right and prudent; for beyond the grave
There is another world! and call to mind,
Ere your decrees proclaim to all mankind
Murder is legalized, that there the Slave
Before the Eternal, 'thunder-tongued shall plead
Against the deep damnation of your deed.'

ROBERT SOUTHEY   147

TO TOUSSAINT L'OUVERTURE

[*On hearing of the imprisonment of Toussaint, leader of
the Haitian revolution, for resisting Napoleon's reimposition
of slavery*]

Toussaint, the most unhappy Man of Men!
Whether the rural Milk-maid by her Cow
Sing in thy hearing, or thou liest now
Alone in some deep dungeon's earless den,
O miserable chieftain! where and when
Wilt thou find patience? Yet die not; do thou
Wear rather in thy bonds a chearful brow:
Though fallen Thyself, never to rise again,
Live, and take comfort. Thou hast left behind
Powers that will work for thee; air, earth, and skies;
There's not a breathing of the common wind
That will forget thee; thou hast great allies;
Thy friends are exultations, agonies,
And love, and Man's unconquerable mind.

from THE PRELUDE:
RESIDENCE IN FRANCE

Hatred of absolute rule, where will of one
Is law for all, and of that barren pride
In them who, by immunities unjust,
Between the sovereign and the people stand,
His helper and not theirs, laid stronger hold
Daily upon me, mixed with pity too
And love; for where hope is, there love will be
For the abject multitude. And when we chanced
One day to meet a hunger-bitten girl,
Who crept along fitting her languid gait
Unto a heifer's motion, by a cord
Tied to her arm, and picking thus from the lane
Its sustenance, while the girl with pallid hands
Was busy knitting in a heartless mood
Of solitude, and at the sight my friend
In agitation said, ''Tis against *that*
That we are fighting,' I with him believed
That a benignant spirit was abroad
Which might not be withstood, that poverty
Abject as this would in a little time
Be found no more, that we should see the earth
Unthwarted in her wish to recompense
The meek, the lowly, patient child of toil,
All institutes for ever blotted out

That legalized exclusion, empty pomp
Abolished, sensual state and cruel power,
Whether by edict of the one or few;
And finally, as sum and crown of all,
Should see the people having a strong hand
In framing their own laws; whence better days
To all mankind. But, these things set apart,
Was not this single confidence enough
To animate the mind that ever turned
A thought to human welfare?

TO A FRIEND

Composed near Calais, on the road leading to Ardres,
August 7th, 1802

Jones! when from Calais southward you and I
Travell'd on foot together, then this way,
Which I am pacing now, was like the May
With festivals of new-born Liberty:
A homeless sound of joy was in the Sky;
The antiquated Earth, as one might say,
Beat like the heart of Man: songs, garlands, play,
Banners, and happy faces, far and nigh!
And now, sole register that these things were,
Two solitary greetings have I heard,
'Good-morrow, Citizen!' a hollow word,
As if a dead man spake it! Yet despair
I feel not: happy am I as a bird:
Fair seasons yet will come, and hopes as fair.

COMPOSED BY THE SEA-SIDE,
NEAR CALAIS

Fair Star of evening, Splendour of the West,
Star of my Country! on the horizon's brink
Thou hangest, stooping, as might seem, to sink
On England's bosom; yet well pleas'd to rest,
Meanwhile, and be to her a glorious crest
Conspicuous to the Nations. Thou, I think,
Should'st be my Country's emblem; and
    should'st wink,
Bright Star! with laughter on her banners, drest
In thy fresh beauty. There! that dusky spot
Beneath thee, it is England; there it lies.
Blessings be on you both! one hope, one lot,
One life, one glory! I, with many a fear
For my dear Country, many heartfelt sighs,
Among men who do not love her linger here.

from THE MASK OF ANARCHY
Written on the occasion of the massacre at Manchester

As I lay asleep in Italy,
There came a voice from over the sea,
And with great power it forth led me
To walk in the visions of Poesy.

I met Murder on the way –
He had a mask like Castlereagh –
Very smooth he looked, yet grim;
Seven bloodhounds followed him:

All were fat; and well they might
Be in admirable plight,
For one by one, and two by two,
He tossed them human hearts to chew,
Which from his wide cloak he drew.

Next came Fraud, and he had on,
Like Lord E—, an ermined gown;
His big tears, for he wept well,
Turned to mill-stones as they fell;

And the little children, who
Round his feet played to and fro,
Thinking every tear a gem,
Had their brains knocked out by them.

Clothed with the bible as with light,
And the shadow of the night,
Like S*** next, Hypocrisy,
On a crocodile rode by.

And many more Destructions played
In this ghastly masquerade,
All disguised, even to the eyes,
Like bishops, lawyers, peers, or spies.

Last came Anarchy; he rode
On a white horse splashed with blood;
He was pale even to the lips,
Like Death in the Apocalypse.

And he wore a kingly crown;
And in his grasp a sceptre shone;
On his brow this mark I saw –
'I am God, and King, and Law!'

With a pace stately and fast,
Over English land he passed,
Trampling to a mire of blood
The adoring multitude,

And a mighty troop around,
With their trampling shook the ground,
Waving each a bloody sword,
For the service of their Lord.

And with glorious triumph, they
Rode through England, proud and gay,
Drunk as with intoxication
Of the wine of desolation.

O'er fields and towns, from sea to sea,
Passed the pageant swift and free,
Tearing up, and trampling down;
Till they came to London town.

And each dweller, panic-stricken,
Felt his heart with terror sicken,
Hearing the tempestuous cry
Of the triumph of Anarchy.

For with pomp to meet him came,
Clothed in arms like blood and flame,
The hired murderers, who did sing
'Thou art God, and Law, and King.

'We have waited, weak and lone
For thy coming, Mighty One!
Our purses are empty, our swords are cold,
Give us glory, and blood, and gold.'

Lawyers and priests, a motley crowd,
To the earth their pale brows bowed,
Like a bad prayer not over loud
Whispering – 'Thou art Law and God!'

Then all cried with one accord,
'Thou art King, and God, and Lord;
Anarchy, to thee we bow,
Be thy name made holy now!'

And Anarchy, the skeleton,
Bowed and grinned to every one,
As well as if his education
Had cost ten millions to the nation.

For he knew the palaces
Of our kings were rightly his;
His the sceptre, crown, and globe,
And the gold-inwoven robe.

So he sent his slaves before
To seize upon the Bank and Tower,
And was proceeding with intent
To meet his pensioned parliament

When one fled past, a maniac maid,
And her name was Hope, she said:
But she looked more like Despair;
And she cried out in the air:

'My father Time is weak and grey
With waiting for a better day;
See how idiot-like he stands,
Fumbling with his palsied hands!

'He has had child after child,
And the dust of death is piled
Over every one but me —
Misery! oh, Misery!'

Then she lay down in the street,
Right before the horses' feet,
Expecting, with a patient eye,
Murder, Fraud, and Anarchy.

When between her and her foes
A mist, a light, an image rose,
Small at first, and weak and frail
Like the vapour of the vale:

Till as clouds grow on the blast,
Like tower-crowned giants striding fast,
And glare with lightnings as they fly,
And speak in thunder to the sky,

It grew – a shape arrayed in mail
Brighter than the viper's scale,
And upborne on wings whose grain
Was as the light of sunny rain.

On its helm, seen far away,
A planet, like the morning's, lay;
And those plumes its light rained through
Like a shower of crimson dew.

With step as soft as wind it passed,
O'er the heads of men – so fast
That they knew the presence there,
And looked – and all was empty air.

As flowers beneath May's footstep waken,
As stars from night's loose hair are shaken,
As waves arise when loud winds call,
Thoughts sprung where'er that step did fall.

And the prostrate multitude
Looked – and ankle-deep in blood,
Hope, that maiden most serene,
Was walking with a quiet mien:

And Anarchy, the ghastly birth,
Lay dead earth upon the earth;
The Horse of Death tameless as wind,
Fled, and with his hoofs did grind
To dust the murderers thronged behind.

A rushing light of clouds and splendour,
A sense, awakening and yet tender,
Was heard and felt – and at its close
These words of joy and fear arose:

As if their own indignant earth,
Which gave the sons of England birth,
Had felt their blood upon her brow,
And shuddering with a mother's throe,

Had turned every drop of blood,
By which her face had been bedewed,
To an accent unwithstood,
As if her heart had cried aloud:

'Men of England, heirs of Glory,
Heroes of unwritten story,
Nurslings of one mighty mother,
Hopes of her, and one another!

'Rise, like lions after slumber,
In unvanquishable number,
Shake your chains to earth like dew,
Which in sleep had fall'n on you.
Ye are many, they are few.'

ENGLAND IN 1819

An old, mad, blind, despised, and dying King;
Princes, the dregs of their dull race, who flow
Through public scorn,– mud from a muddy spring;
Rulers who neither see nor feel nor know,
But leechlike to their fainting country cling
Till they drop, blind in blood, without a blow.
A people starved and stabbed in th' untilled field;
An army, whom liberticide and prey
Makes as a two-edged sword to all who wield;
Golden and sanguine laws which tempt and slay;
Religion Christless, Godless – a book sealed;
A senate, Time's worst statute, unrepealed –
Are graves from which a glorious Phantom may
Burst, to illumine our tempestuous day.

PERCY BYSSHE SHELLEY   161

THE FALLEN ELM

Old elm that murmured in our chimney top
The sweetest anthem autumn ever made
And into mellow whispering calms would drop
When showers fell on thy many-coloured shade
And when dark tempests mimic thunder made
While darkness came as it would strangle light
With the black tempest of a winter night
That rocked thee like a cradle to thy root,
How did I love to hear the winds upbraid
Thy strength without – while all within was mute.
It seasoned comfort to our hearts' desire,
We felt thy kind protection like a friend
And edged our chairs up closer to the fire,
Enjoying comforts that was never penned.
Old favourite tree, thou'st seen time's changes lower,
Though change till now did never injure thee,
For time beheld thee as her sacred dower
And nature claimed thee her domestic tree;
Storms came and shook thee many a weary hour,
Yet steadfast to thy home thy roots hath been;
Summers of thirst parched round thy homely bower
Till earth grew iron – still thy leaves was green.
The children sought thee in thy summer shade
And made their playhouse rings of stick and stone;
The mavis sang and felt himself alone

While in thy leaves his early nest was made
And I did feel his happiness mine own,
Nought heeding that our friendship was betrayed,
Friend not inanimate – though stocks and stones
There are and many formed of flesh and bones,
Thou owned a language by which hearts are stirred
Deeper than by a feeling clothed in words,
And speakest now what's known of every tongue,
Language of pity and the force of wrong.
What cant assumes, what hypocrites will dare,
Speaks home to truth and shows it what they are.
I see a picture which thy fate displays
And learn a lesson from thy destiny:
Self-interest saw thee stand in freedom's ways,
So thy old shadow must a tyrant be;
Thou'st heard the knave abusing those in power,
Bawl freedom loud and then oppress the free;
Thou'st sheltered hypocrites in many a shower
That when in power would never shelter thee;
Thou'st heard the knave supply his canting powers
With wrong's illusions when he wanted friends
That bawled for shelter when he lived in showers
And when clouds vanished made thy shade amends –
With axe at root he felled thee to the ground
And barked of freedom – O, I hate the sound!
Time hears its visions speak and age sublime
Hath made thee a disciple unto time.

It grows the cant term of enslaving tools
To wrong another by the name of right;
It grows the licence of o'erbearing fools
To cheat plain honesty by force of might.
Thus came enclosure – ruin was its guide,
But freedom's clapping hands enjoyed the sight
Though comfort's cottage soon was thrust aside
And workhouse prisons raised upon the site.
E'en nature's dwellings far away from men –
The common heath – became the spoiler's prey:
The rabbit had not where to make his den
And labour's only cow was drove away.
No matter – wrong was right and right was wrong
And freedom's bawl was sanction to the song.
– Such was thy ruin, music-making elm:
The rights of freedom was to injure thine.
As thou wert served, so would they overwhelm
In freedom's name the little that is mine.
And there are knaves that brawl for better laws
And cant of tyranny in stronger powers,
Who glut their vile unsatiated maws
And freedom's birthright from the weak devours.

from AUGURIES OF INNOCENCE

To see a World in a Grain of Sand
And a Heaven in a Wild Flower
Hold Infinity in the palm of your hand
And Eternity in an hour
A Robin Red breast in a Cage
Puts all Heaven in a Rage
A Dove house fill'd with Doves & Pigeons
Shudders Hell thro' all its regions
A dog starv'd at his Master's Gate
Predicts the ruin of the State
A Horse misus'd upon the Road
Calls to Heaven for Human blood
Each outcry of the hunted Hare
A fibre from the Brain does tear
A Skylark wounded in the wing
A Cherubim does cease to sing

* * *

The Whore & Gambler by the State
Licenc'd build that Nation's Fate
The Harlot's cry from Street to Street
Shall weave Old England's winding Sheet
The Winner's Shout the Loser's Curse
Dance before dead England's Hearse

Every Night & every Morn
Some to Misery are Born
Every Morn & every Night
Some are Born to sweet delight
Some are Born to sweet delight
Some are Born to Endless Night
We are led to Believe a Lie
When we see not Thro the Eye
Which was Born in a Night to perish in a Night
When the Soul Slept in Beams of Light
God Appears & God is Light
To those poor Souls who dwell in Night
But does a Human Form Display
To those who Dwell in Realms of day

RESOLUTION AND INDEPENDENCE

There was a roaring in the wind all night;
The rain came heavily and fell in floods;
But now the sun is rising calm and bright;
The birds are singing in the distant woods;
Over his own sweet voice the stock-dove broods;
The jay makes answer as the magpie chatters;
And all the air is filled with pleasant noise of waters.

All things that love the sun are out of doors;
The sky rejoices in the morning's birth;
The grass is bright with rain-drops; on the moors
The hare is running races in her mirth;
And with her feet she from the plashy earth
Raises a mist; which, glittering in the sun,
Runs with her all the way, wherever she doth run.

I was a traveller then upon the moor;
I saw the hare that raced about with joy;
I heard the woods and distant waters roar;
Or heard them not, as happy as a boy:
The pleasant season did my heart employ:
My old remembrances went from me wholly;
And all the ways of men, so vain and melancholy.

But, as it sometimes chanceth, from the might
Of joys in minds that can no farther go,
As high as we have mounted in delight
In our dejection do we sink as low;
To me that morning did it happen so;
And fears and fancies thick upon me came;
Dim sadness and blind thoughts I knew not nor
      could name.

I heard the sky-lark warbling in the sky;
And I bethought me of the playful hare:
Even such a happy child of earth am I;
Even as these blissful creatures do I fare;
Far from the world I walk, and from all care;
But there may come another day to me,
Solitude, pain of heart, distress, and poverty.

My whole life I have lived in pleasant thought,
As if life's business were a summer mood;
As if all needful things would come unsought
To genial faith, still rich in genial good;
But how can he expect that others should
Build for him, sow for him, and at his call
Love him, who for himself will take no heed at all?

I thought of Chatterton, the marvellous boy,
The sleepless soul that perished in its pride;
Of him who walked in glory and in joy
Behind his plough, along the mountain-side:
By our own spirits are we deified;
We poets in our youth begin in gladness;
But thereof come in the end despondency and
 madness.

Now, whether it were by peculiar grace,
A leading from above, a something given,
Yet it befell that, in this lonely place,
When up and down my fancy thus was driven,
And I with these untoward thoughts had striven,
I saw a man before me unawares:
The oldest man he seemed that ever wore grey hairs.

My course I stopped as soon as I espied
The old man in that naked wilderness:
Close by a pond, upon the further side,
He stood alone: a minute's space I guess
I watched him, he continuing motionless:
To the pool's further margin then I drew;
He being all the while before me full in view.

As a huge stone is sometimes seen to lie
Couched on the bald top of an eminence;
Wonder to all who do the same espy,
By what means it could thither come, and whence;
So that it seems a thing endued with sense:
Like a sea-beast crawled forth, which on a shelf
Of rock or sand reposeth, there to sun itself.

Such seemed this man, not all alive nor dead,
Nor all asleep; in his extreme old age:
His body was bent double, feet and head
Coming together in their pilgrimage;
As if some dire constraint of pain, or rage
Of sickness felt by him in times long past,
A more than human weight upon his frame had cast.

Himself he propped, limbs, body, and face,
Upon a long grey staff of shaven wood:
And, still as I drew near with gentle pace,
Beside the little pond or moorish flood
Motionless as a cloud the old man stood,
That heareth not the loud winds when they call,
And moveth altogether, if it move at all.

At length, himself unsettling, he the pond
Stirred with his staff, and fixedly did look
Upon the muddy water, which he conned,
As if he had been reading in a book:
And now such freedom as I could I took;
And, drawing to his side, to him did say,
'This morning gives us promise of a glorious day.'

A gentle answer did the old man make,
In courteous speech which forth he slowly drew:
And him with further words I thus bespake,
'What kind of work is that which you pursue?
This is a lonesome place for one like you.'
He answered me with pleasure and surprise;
And there was, while he spake, a fire about his eyes.

His words came feebly, from a feeble chest,
Yet each in solemn order followed each,
With something of a lofty utterance dressed;
Choice word and measured phrase, above the reach
Of ordinary men; a stately speech!
Such as grave livers do in Scotland use,
Religious men, who give to God and man their dues.

He told me that he to this pond had come
To gather leeches, being old and poor:
Employment hazardous and wearisome!
And he had many hardships to endure:
From pond to pond he roamed, from moor to moor,
Housing, with God's good help, by choice or chance;
And in this way he gained an honest maintenance.

The old man still stood talking by my side;
But now his voice to me was like a stream
Scarce heard; nor word from word could I divide;
And the whole body of the man did seem
Like one whom I had met with in a dream;
Or like a man from some far region sent,
To give me human strength, and strong
    admonishment.

My former thoughts returned: the fear that kills;
And hope that is unwilling to be fed;
Cold, pain, and labour, and all fleshly ills;
And mighty poets in their misery dead.
And now, not knowing what the old man had said,
My question eagerly did I renew,
'How is it that you live, and what is it you do?'

He with a smile did then his words repeat;
And said that, gathering leeches, far and wide
He travelled; stirring thus about his feet
The waters of the ponds where they abide.
'Once I could meet with them on every side;
But they have dwindled long by slow decay;
Yet still I persevere, and find them where I may.'

While he was talking thus, the lonely place,
The old man's shape, and speech, all troubled me:
In my mind's eye I seemed to see him pace
About the weary moors continually,
Wandering about alone and silently.
While I these thoughts within myself pursued,
He, having made a pause, the same discourse renewed.

And soon with this he other matter blended,
Cheerfully uttered, with demeanour kind,
But stately in the main; and, when he ended,
I could have laughed myself to scorn to find
In that decrepit man so firm a mind.
'God,' said I, 'be my help and stay secure;
I'll think of the leech-gatherer on the lonely moor.'

PREFACE TO *MILTON*

And did those feet in ancient time
Walk upon England's mountains green:
And was the holy Lamb of God,
On England's pleasant pastures seen!

And did the Countenance Divine,
Shine forth upon our clouded hills?
And was Jerusalem builded here,
Among these dark Satanic Mills?

Bring me my Bow of burning gold:
Bring me my Arrows of desire:
Bring me my Spear: O clouds unfold!
Bring me my Chariot of fire!

I will not cease from Mental Fight,
Nor shall my Sword sleep in my hand:
Till we have built Jerusalem,
In England's green & pleasant Land.

LOVE

SHE WALKS IN BEAUTY, LIKE THE NIGHT

She walks in beauty, like the night
  Of cloudless climes and starry skies;
And all that's best of dark and bright
  Meet in her aspect and her eyes;
Thus mellowed to that tender light
  Which heaven to gaudy day denies.

One shade the more, one ray the less,
  Had half impaired the nameless grace
Which waves in every raven tress,
  Or softly lightens o'er her face;
Where thoughts serenely sweet express,
  How pure, how dear their dwelling-place.

And on that cheek, and o'er that brow,
  So soft, so calm, yet eloquent,
The smiles that win, the tints that glow,
  But tell of days in goodness spent,
A mind at peace with all below,
  A heart whose love is innocent!

from MARMION: THE ARRIVAL OF LOCHINVAR

O, young Lochinvar is come out of the west,
Through all the wide Border his steed was the best;
And save his good broadsword he weapons had none,
He rode all unarm'd, and he rode all alone.
So faithful in love, and so dauntless in war,
There never was knight like the young Lochinvar.

He staid not for brake, and he stopp'd not for stone,
He swam the Eske river where ford there was none;
But ere he alighted at Netherby gate,
The bride had consented, the gallant came late:
For a laggard in love, and a dastard in war,
Was to wed the fair Ellen of brave Lochinvar.

So boldly he enter'd the Netherby Hall,
Among bride's-men, and kinsmen, and brothers
        and all:
Then spoke the bride's father, his hand on his sword,
(For the poor craven bridegroom said never a word,)
'O come ye in peace here, or come ye in war,
Or to dance at our bridal, young Lord Lochinvar?'

'I long woo'd your daughter, my suit you denied;—
Love swells like the Solway, but ebbs like its tide –
And now I am come, with this lost love of mine,
To lead but one measure, drink one cup of wine.
There are maidens in Scotland more lovely by far,
That would gladly be bride to the young Lochinvar.'

The bride kiss'd the goblet: the knight took it up,
He quaff'd off the wine, and he threw down the cup.
She look'd down to blush, and she look'd up to sigh,
With a smile on her lips and a tear in her eye.
He took her soft hand, ere her mother could bar,—
'Now tread we a measure!' said young Lochinvar.

So stately his form, and so lovely her face,
That never a hall such a galliard did grace;
While her mother did fret, and her father did fume,
And the bridegroom stood dangling his bonnet
        and plume;
And the bride-maidens whisper'd, "Twere better
        by far
To have match'd our fair cousin with young
        Lochinvar.'

One touch to her hand, and one word in her ear,
When they reach'd the hall-door, and the charger
    stood near;
So light to the croupe the fair lady he swung,
So light to the saddle before her he sprung! –
'She is won! we are gone, over bank, bush, and scaur;
They'll have fleet steeds that follow,' quoth young
    Lochinvar.

There was mounting 'mong Graemes of the Netherby
    clan;
Forsters, Fenwicks, and Musgraves, they rode and
    they ran;
There was racing and chasing on Cannobie Lee,
But the lost bride of Netherby ne'er did they see.
So daring in love, and so dauntless in war,
Have ye e'er heard of gallant like young Lochinvar?

THE EVE OF ST. AGNES

St. Agnes' Eve – Ah, bitter chill it was!
The owl, for all his feathers, was a-cold;
The hare limp'd trembling through the frozen grass,
And silent was the flock in woolly fold:
Numb were the Beadsman's fingers, while he told
His rosary, and while his frosted breath,
Like pious incense from a censer old,
Seem'd taking flight for heaven, without a death,
Past the sweet Virgin's picture, while his prayer
    he saith.

His prayer he saith, this patient, holy man;
Then takes his lamp, and riseth from his knees,
And back returneth, meagre, barefoot, wan,
Along the chapel aisle by slow degrees:
The sculptur'd dead, on each side, seem to freeze,
Emprison'd in black, purgatorial rails:
Knights, ladies, praying in dumb orat'ries,
He passeth by; and his weak spirit fails
To think how they may ache in icy hoods and mails.

Northward he turneth through a little door,
And scarce three steps, ere Music's golden tongue
Flatter'd to tears this aged man and poor;
But no – already had his deathbell rung;

The joys of all his life were said and sung:
His was harsh penance on St. Agnes' Eve:
Another way he went, and soon among
Rough ashes sat he for his soul's reprieve,
And all night kept awake, for sinners' sake to grieve.

That ancient Beadsman heard the prelude soft;
And so it chanc'd, for many a door was wide,
From hurry to and fro. Soon, up aloft,
The silver, snarling trumpets 'gan to chide:
The level chambers, ready with their pride,
Were glowing to receive a thousand guests:
The carved angels, ever eager-eyed,
Star'd, where upon their heads the cornice rests,
With hair blown back, and wings put cross-wise on
      their breasts.

At length burst in the argent revelry,
With plume, tiara, and all rich array,
Numerous as shadows haunting fairily
The brain, new stuff'd, in youth, with triumphs gay
Of old romance. These let us wish away,
And turn, sole-thoughted, to one Lady there,
Whose heart had brooded, all that wintry day,
On love, and wing'd St. Agnes' saintly care,
As she had heard old dames full many times declare.

They told her how, upon St. Agnes' Eve,
Young virgins might have visions of delight,
And soft adorings from their loves receive
Upon the honey'd middle of the night,
If ceremonies due they did aright;
As, supperless to bed they must retire,
And couch supine their beauties, lily white;
Nor look behind, nor sideways, but require
Of Heaven with upward eyes for all that they desire.

Full of this whim was thoughtful Madeline:
The music, yearning like a God in pain,
She scarcely heard: her maiden eyes divine,
Fix'd on the floor, saw many a sweeping train
Pass by – she heeded not at all: in vain
Came many a tiptoe, amorous cavalier,
And back retir'd; not cool'd by high disdain,
But she saw not: her heart was otherwhere:
She sigh'd for Agnes' dreams, the sweetest of the year.

She danc'd along with vague, regardless eyes,
Anxious her lips, her breathing quick and short:
The hallow'd hour was near at hand: she sighs
Amid the timbrels, and the throng'd resort
Of whisperers in anger, or in sport;
'Mid looks of love, defiance, hate, and scorn,
Hoodwink'd with faery fancy; all amort,

Save to St. Agnes and her lambs unshorn,
And all the bliss to be before to-morrow morn.

So, purposing each moment to retire,
She linger'd still. Meantime, across the moors,
Had come young Porphyro, with heart on fire
For Madeline. Beside the portal doors,
Buttress'd from moonlight, stands he, and implores
All saints to give him sight of Madeline,
But for one moment in the tedious hours,
That he might gaze and worship all unseen;
Perchance speak, kneel, touch, kiss – in sooth such
        things have been.

He ventures in: let no buzz'd whisper tell:
All eyes be muffled, or a hundred swords
Will storm his heart, Love's fev'rous citadel:
For him, those chambers held barbarian hordes,
Hyena foemen, and hot-blooded lords,
Whose very dogs would execrations howl
Against his lineage: not one breast affords
Him any mercy, in that mansion foul,
Save one old beldame, weak in body and in soul.

Ah, happy chance! the aged creature came,
Shuffling along with ivory-headed wand,
To where he stood, hid from the torch's flame,

Behind a broad hall-pillar, far beyond
The sound of merriment and chorus bland:
He startled her; but soon she knew his face,
And grasp'd his fingers in her palsied hand,
Saying, 'Mercy, Porphyro! hie thee from this place;
They are all here to-night, the whole blood-thirsty
    race!

'Get hence! get hence! there's dwarfish Hildebrand;
He had a fever late, and in the fit
He cursed thee and thine, both house and land:
Then there's that old Lord Maurice, not a whit
More tame for his gray hairs – Alas me! flit!
Flit like a ghost away.' – 'Ah, Gossip dear,
We're safe enough; here in this arm-chair sit,
And tell me how' – 'Good Saints! not here, not here;
Follow me, child, or else these stones will be thy bier.'

He follow'd through a lowly arched way,
Brushing the cobwebs with his lofty plume,
And as she mutter'd 'Well-a–well-a-day!'
He found him in a little moonlight room,
Pale, lattic'd, chill, and silent as a tomb.
'Now tell me where is Madeline,' said he,
'O tell me, Angela, by the holy loom
Which none but secret sisterhood may see,
When they St. Agnes' wool are weaving piously.'

'St. Agnes! Ah! it is St. Agnes' Eve –
Yet men will murder upon holy days:
Thou must hold water in a witch's sieve,
And be liege-lord of all the Elves and Fays,
To venture so: it fills me with amaze
To see thee, Porphyro! – St. Agnes' Eve!
God's help! my lady fair the conjuror plays
This very night: good angels her deceive!
But let me laugh awhile, I've mickle time to grieve.'

Feebly she laugheth in the languid moon,
While Porphyro upon her face doth look,
Like puzzled urchin on an aged crone
Who keepeth clos'd a wond'rous riddle-book,
As spectacled she sits in chimney nook.
But soon his eyes grew brilliant, when she told
His lady's purpose; and he scarce could brook
Tears, at the thought of those enchantments cold,
And Madeline asleep in lap of legends old.

Sudden a thought came like a full-blown rose,
Flushing his brow, and in his pained heart
Made purple riot: then doth he propose
A stratagem, that makes the beldame start:
'A cruel man and impious thou art:
Sweet lady, let her pray, and sleep, and dream
Alone with her good angels, far apart

From wicked men like thee. Go, go! – I deem
Thou canst not surely be the same that thou didst seem.'

'I will not harm her, by all saints I swear,'
Quoth Porphyro: 'O may I ne'er find grace
When my weak voice shall whisper its last prayer,
If one of her soft ringlets I displace,
Or look with ruffian passion in her face:
Good Angela, believe me by these tears;
Or I will, even in a moment's space,
Awake, with horrid shout, my foemen's ears,
And beard them, though they be more fang'd than
     wolves and bears.'

'Ah! why wilt thou affright a feeble soul?
A poor, weak, palsy-stricken, churchyard thing,
Whose passing-bell may ere the midnight toll;
Whose prayers for thee, each morn and evening,
Were never miss'd.' – Thus plaining, doth she bring
A gentler speech from burning Porphyro;
So woeful, and of such deep sorrowing,
That Angela gives promise she will do
Whatever he shall wish, betide her weal or woe.

Which was, to lead him, in close secrecy,
Even to Madeline's chamber, and there hide
Him in a closet, of such privacy

That he might see her beauty unespied,
And win perhaps that night a peerless bride,
While legion'd fairies pac'd the coverlet,
And pale enchantment held her sleepy-eyed.
Never on such a night have lovers met,
Since Merlin paid his Demon all the monstrous debt.

'It shall be as thou wishest,' said the Dame:
'All cates and dainties shall be stored there
Quickly on this feast-night: by the tambour frame
Her own lute thou wilt see: no time to spare,
For I am slow and feeble, and scarce dare
On such a catering trust my dizzy head.
Wait here, my child, with patience; kneel in prayer
The while: Ah! thou must needs the lady wed,
Or may I never leave my grave among the dead.'

So saying, she hobbled off with busy fear.
The lover's endless minutes slowly pass'd;
The dame return'd, and whisper'd in his ear
To follow her; with aged eyes aghast
From fright of dim espial. Safe at last,
Through many a dusky gallery, they gain
The maiden's chamber, silken, hush'd, and chaste;
Where Porphyro took covert, pleas'd amain.
His poor guide hurried back with agues in her brain.

Her falt'ring hand upon the balustrade,
Old Angela was feeling for the stair,
When Madeline, St. Agnes' charmed maid,
Rose, like a mission'd spirit, unaware:
With silver taper's light, and pious care,
She turn'd, and down the aged gossip led
To a safe level matting. Now prepare,
Young Porphyro, for gazing on that bed;
She comes, she comes again, like ring-dove fray'd
    and fled.

Out went the taper as she hurried in;
Its little smoke, in pallid moonshine, died:
She clos'd the door, she panted, all akin
To spirits of the air, and visions wide:
No uttered syllable, or, woe betide!
But to her heart, her heart was voluble,
Paining with eloquence her balmy side;
As though a tongueless nightingale should swell
Her throat in vain, and die, heart-stifled, in her dell.

A casement high and triple-arch'd there was,
All garlanded with carven imag'ries
Of fruits, and flowers, and bunches of knot-grass,
And diamonded with panes of quaint device,
Innumerable of stains and splendid dyes,
As are the tiger-moth's deep-damask'd wings;

And in the midst, 'mong thousand heraldries,
And twilight saints, and dim emblazonings,
A shielded scutcheon blush'd with blood of queens
    and kings.

Full on this casement shone the wintry moon,
And threw warm gules on Madeline's fair breast,
As down she knelt for heaven's grace and boon;
Rose-bloom fell on her hands, together pressed,
And on her silver cross soft amethyst,
And on her hair a glory, like a saint:
She seem'd a splendid angel, newly dressed,
Save wings, for heaven:– Porphyro grew faint:
She knelt, so pure a thing, so free from mortal taint.

Anon his heart revives: her vespers done,
Of all its wreathed pearls her hair she frees;
Unclasps her warmed jewels one by one;
Loosens her fragrant boddice; by degrees
Her rich attire creeps rustling to her knees:
Half-hidden, like a mermaid in sea-weed,
Pensive awhile she dreams awake, and sees,
In fancy, fair St. Agnes in her bed,
But dares not look behind, or all the charm is fled.

Soon, trembling in her soft and chilly nest,
In sort of wakeful swoon, perplex'd she lay,

Until the poppied warmth of sleep oppress'd
Her soothed limbs, and soul fatigued away;
Flown, like a thought, until the morrow-day;
Blissfully haven'd both from joy and pain;
Clasp'd like a missal where swart Paynims pray;
Blinded alike from sunshine and from rain,
As though a rose should shut, and be a bud again.

Stol'n to this paradise, and so entranced,
Porphyro gazed upon her empty dress,
And listen'd to her breathing, if it chanced
To wake into a slumberous tenderness;
Which when he heard, that minute did he bless,
And breath'd himself: then from the closet crept,
Noiseless as fear in a wide wilderness,
And over the hush'd carpet, silent, stepped,
And 'tween the curtains peep'd, where, lo! – how fast
    she slept.

Then by the bed-side, where the faded moon
Made a dim, silver twilight, soft he set
A table, and, half anguish'd, threw thereon
A cloth of woven crimson, gold, and jet:–
O for some drowsy Morphean amulet!
The boisterous, midnight, festive clarion,
The kettle-drum, and far-heard clarinet,

Affray his ears, though but in dying tone:—
The hall door shuts again, and all the noise is gone.

And still she slept an azure-lidded sleep,
In blanched linen, smooth, and lavender'd,
While he forth from the closet brought a heap
Of candied apple, quince, and plum, and gourd;
With jellies soother than the creamy curd,
And lucent syrops, tinct with cinnamon;
Manna and dates, in argosy transferr'd
From Fez; and spiced dainties, every one,
From silken Samarcand to cedar'd Lebanon.

These delicates he heap'd with glowing hand
On golden dishes and in baskets bright
Of wreathed silver: sumptuous they stand
In the retired quiet of the night,
Filling the chilly room with perfume light.—
'And now, my love, my seraph fair, awake!
Thou art my heaven, and I thine eremite:
Open thine eyes, for meek St. Agnes' sake,
Or I shall drowse beside thee, so my soul doth ache.'

Thus whispering, his warm, unnerved arm
Sank in her pillow. Shaded was her dream
By the dusk curtains:— 'twas a midnight charm
Impossible to melt as iced stream:

The lustrous salvers in the moonlight gleam;
Broad golden fringe upon the carpet lies:
It seem'd he never, never could redeem
From such a steadfast spell his lady's eyes;
So mus'd awhile, entoil'd in woofed phantasies.

Awakening up, he took her hollow lute,–
Tumultuous,– and, in chords that tenderest be,
He play'd an ancient ditty, long since mute,
In Provence call'd, 'La belle dame sans mercy':
Close to her ear touching the melody;–
Wherewith disturb'd, she utter'd a soft moan:
He ceas'd – she panted quick – and suddenly
Her blue affrayed eyes wide open shone:
Upon his knees he sank, pale as smooth-sculptured
        stone.

Her eyes were open, but she still beheld,
Now wide awake, the vision of her sleep:
There was a painful change, that nigh expell'd
The blisses of her dream so pure and deep
At which fair Madeline began to weep,
And moan forth witless words with many a sigh;
While still her gaze on Porphyro would keep;
Who knelt, with joined hands and piteous eye,
Fearing to move or speak, she look'd so dreamingly.

'Ah, Porphyro!' said she, 'but even now
Thy voice was at sweet tremble in mine ear,
Made tuneable with every sweetest vow;
And those sad eyes were spiritual and clear:
How chang'd thou art! how pallid, chill, and drear!
Give me that voice again, my Porphyro,
Those looks immortal, those complainings dear!
Oh leave me not in this eternal woe,
For if thy diest, my Love, I know not where to go.'

Beyond a mortal man impassion'd far
At these voluptuous accents, he arose
Ethereal, flush'd, and like a throbbing star
Seen mid the sapphire heaven's deep repose;
Into her dream he melted, as the rose
Blendeth its odour with the violet,—
Solution sweet: meantime the frost-wind blows
Like Love's alarum pattering the sharp sleet
Against the window-panes; St. Agnes' moon hath set.

'Tis dark: quick pattereth the flaw-blown sleet:
'This is no dream, my bride, my Madeline!'
'Tis dark: the iced gusts still rave and beat:
'No dream, alas! alas! and woe is mine!
Porphyro will leave me here to fade and pine.—
Cruel! what traitor could thee hither bring?
I curse not, for my heart is lost in thine,

Though thou forsakest a deceived thing;–
A dove forlorn and lost with sick unpruned wing.'

'My Madeline! sweet dreamer! lovely bride!
Say, may I be for aye thy vassal blest?
Thy beauty's shield, heart-shap'd and vermeil dyed?
Ah, silver shrine, here will I take my rest
After so many hours of toil and quest,
A famish'd pilgrim,– saved by miracle.
Though I have found, I will not rob thy nest
Saving of thy sweet self; if thou think'st well
To trust, fair Madeline, to no rude infidel.

'Hark! 'tis an elfin-storm from faery land,
Of haggard seeming, but a boon indeed:
Arise – arise! the morning is at hand;–
The bloated wassaillers will never heed:–
Let us away, my love, with happy speed;
There are no ears to hear, or eyes to see,–
Drown'd all in Rhenish and the sleepy mead:
Awake! arise! my love, and fearless be,
For o'er the southern moors I have a home for thee.'

She hurried at his words, beset with fears,
For there were sleeping dragons all around,
At glaring watch, perhaps, with ready spears –
Down the wide stairs a darkling way they found.–

In all the house was heard no human sound.
A chain-droop'd lamp was flickering by each door;
The arras, rich with horseman, hawk, and hound,
Flutter'd in the besieging wind's uproar;
And the long carpets rose along the gusty floor.

They glide, like phantoms, into the wide hall;
Like phantoms, to the iron porch, they glide;
Where lay the Porter, in uneasy sprawl,
With a huge empty flagon by his side:
The wakeful bloodhound rose, and shook his hide,
But his sagacious eye an inmate owns:
By one, and one, the bolts full easy slide:–
The chains lie silent on the footworn stones;–
The key turns, and the door upon its hinges groans.

And they are gone: ay, ages long ago
These lovers fled away into the storm.
That night the Baron dreamt of many a woe,
And all his warrior-guests, with shade and form
Of witch, and demon, and large coffin-worm,
Were long be-nightmar'd. Angela the old
Died palsy-twitch'd, with meagre face deform;
The Beadsman, after thousand aves told,
For aye unsought for slept among his ashes cold.

from DON JUAN

It was the cooling hour, just when the rounded
   Red sun sinks down behind the azure hill,
Which then seems as if the whole earth it bounded,
   Circling all nature, hush'd, and dim, and still,
With the far mountain-crescent half surrounded
   On one side, and the deep sea calm and chill
Upon the other, and the rosy sky,
With one star sparkling through it like an eye.

And thus they wander'd forth, and hand in hand,
   Over the shining pebbles and the shells,
Glided along the smooth and harden'd sand,
   And in the worn and wild receptacles
Work'd by the storms, yet work'd as it were plann'd,
   In hollow halls, with sparry roofs and cells,
They turn'd to rest; and, each clasp'd by an arm,
Yielded to the deep twilight's purple charm.

They look'd up to the sky, whose floating glow
  Spread like a rosy ocean, vast and bright;
They gazed upon the glittering sea below,
  Whence the broad moon rose circling into sight;
They heard the wave's splash, and the wind so low,
  And saw each other's dark eyes darting light
Into each other – and, beholding this,
Their lips drew near, and clung into a kiss;

A long, long kiss, a kiss of youth, and love,
  And beauty, all concentrating like rays
Into one focus, kindled from above;
  Such kisses as belong to early days,
Where heart, and soul, and sense, in concert move,
  And the blood's lava, and the pulse a blaze,
Each kiss a heart-quake,– for a kiss's strength,
I think it must be reckon'd by its length.

By length I mean duration; theirs endured
  Heaven knows how long – no doubt they never
      reckon'd;
And if they had, they could not have secured
  The sum of their sensations to a second:
They had not spoken; but they felt allured,
  As if their souls and lips each other beckon'd,
Which, being join'd, like swarming bees they clung –
Their hearts the flowers from whence the honey sprung.

They were alone, but not alone as they
　　Who shut in chambers think it loneliness;
The silent ocean, and the starlight bay,
　　The twilight glow which momently grew less,
The voiceless sands, and dropping caves, that lay
　　Around them, made them to each other press,
As if there were no life beneath the sky
Save theirs, and that their life could never die.

They fear'd no eyes nor ears on that lone beach,
　　They felt no terrors from the night, they were
All in all to each other; though their speech
　　Was broken words, they *thought* a language there,–
And all the burning tongues the passions teach
　　Found in one sigh the best interpreter
Of nature's oracle – first love,– that all
Which Eve has left her daughters since her fall.

Haidée spoke not of scruples, ask'd no vows,
　　Nor offer'd any; she had never heard
Of plight and promises to be a spouse,
　　Or perils by a loving maid incurr'd;
She was all which pure ignorance allows,
　　And flew to her young mate like a young bird,
And, never having dreamt of falsehood, she
Had not one word to say of constancy.

She loved, and was beloved – she adored,
    And she was worshipp'd; after nature's fashion,
Their intense souls, into each other pour'd,
    If souls could die, had perish'd in that passion,–
But by degrees their senses were restored,
    Again to be o'ercome, again to dash on;
And, beating 'gainst his bosom, Haidée's heart
Felt as if never more to beat apart.

Alas! they were so young, so beautiful,
    So lonely, loving, helpless, and the hour
Was that in which the heart is always full,
    And, having o'er itself no further power,
Prompts deeds eternity can not annul,
    But pays off moments in an endless shower
Of hell-fire – all prepared for people giving
Pleasure or pain to one another living.

Alas! for Juan and Haidée! they were
    So loving and so lovely – till then never,
Excepting our first parents, such a pair
    Had run the risk of being damn'd for ever;
And Haidée, being devout as well as fair,
    Had, doubtless, heard about the Stygian river,
And hell and purgatory – but forgot
Just in the very crisis she should not.

They look upon each other, and their eyes
   Gleam in the moonlight; and her white arm clasps
Round Juan's head, and his around her lies
   Half buried in the tresses which it grasps;
She sits upon his knee, and drinks his sighs,
   He hers, until they end in broken gasps;
And thus they form a group that's quite antique,
Half naked, loving, natural, and Greek.

And when those deep and burning moments pass'd,
   And Juan sunk to sleep within her arms,
She slept not, but all tenderly, though fast,
   Sustain'd his head upon her bosom's charms;
And now and then her eye to heaven is cast,
   And then on the pale cheek her breast now warms,
Pillow'd on her o'erflowing heart, which pants
With all it granted, and with all it grants.

An infant when it gazes on a light,
   A child the moment when it drains the breast,
A devotee when soars the Host in sight,
   An Arab with a stranger for a guest,
A sailor when the prize has struck in fight,
   A miser filling his most hoarded chest,
Feel rapture; but not such true joy are reaping
As they who watch o'er what they love while sleeping.

For there it lies so tranquil, so beloved,
    All that it hath of life with us is living;
So gentle, stirless, helpless, and unmoved,
    And all unconscious of the joy 'tis giving;
All it hath felt, inflicted, pass'd, and proved,
    Hush'd into depths beyond the watcher's diving:
There lies the thing we love with all its errors
And all its charms, like death without its terrors.

The lady watch'd her lover – and that hour
    Of Love's, and Night's, and Ocean's solitude,
O'erflow'd her soul with their united power;
    Amidst the barren sand and rocks so rude
She and her wave-worn love had made their bower,
    Where nought upon their passion could intrude,
And all the stars that crowded the blue space
Saw nothing happier than her glowing face.

Alas! the love of women! it is known
    To be a lovely and a fearful thing;
For all of theirs upon that die is thrown,
    And if 'tis lost, life hath no more to bring
To them but mockeries of the past alone,
    And their revenge is as the tiger's spring,
Deadly, and quick, and crushing; yet, as real
Torture is theirs, what they inflict they feel.

They are right; for man, to man so oft unjust,
   Is always so to women; one sole bond
Awaits them, treachery is all their trust;
   Taught to conceal, their bursting hearts despond
Over their idol, till some wealthier lust
   Buys them in marriage – and what rests beyond?
A thankless husband, next a faithless lover,
Then dressing, nursing, praying, and all's over.

Some take a lover, some take drams or prayers,
   Some mind their household, others dissipation,
Some run away, and but exchange their cares,
   Losing the advantage of a virtuous station;
Few changes e'er can better their affairs,
   Theirs being an unnatural situation,
From the dull palace to the dirty hovel:
Some play the devil, and then write a novel.

Haidée was Nature's bride, and knew not this;
   Haidée was Passion's child, born where the sun
Showers triple light, and scorches even the kiss
   Of his gazelle-eyed daughters; she was one
Made but to love, to feel that she was his
   Who was her chosen: what was said or done
Elsewhere was nothing. She had naught to fear,
Hope, care, nor love, beyond,– her heart beat *here*.

And oh! that quickening of the heart, that beat!
  How much it costs us! yet each rising throb
Is in its cause as its effect so sweet,
  That Wisdom, ever on the watch to rob
Joy of its alchemy, and to repeat
  Fine truths; even Conscience, too, has a tough job
To make us understand each good old maxim,
So good – I wonder Castlereagh don't tax 'em.

And now 'twas done – on the lone shore were plighted
  Their hearts; the stars, their nuptial torches, shed
Beauty upon the beautiful they lighted:
  Ocean their witness, and the cave their bed,
By their own feelings hallow'd and united,
  Their priest was Solitude, and they were wed:
And they were happy, for to their young eyes
Each was an angel, and earth paradise.

SO WE'LL GO NO MORE A ROVING

So we'll go no more a roving
  So late into the night,
Though the heart be still as loving,
  And the moon be still as bright.

For the sword outwears its sheath,
  And the soul wears out the breast,
And the heart must pause to breathe,
  And Love itself have rest.

Though the night was made for loving,
  And the day returns too soon,
Yet we'll go no more a roving
  By the light of the moon.

LORD BYRON

ALONE IN CROWDS TO WANDER ON

Alone in crowds to wander on,
And feel that all the charm is gone
Which voices dear and eyes beloved
Shed round us once, where'er we roved –
This, this the doom must be
Of all who've loved, and lived to see
The few bright things they thought would stay
For ever near them, die away.

Though fairer forms around us throng,
Their smiles to others all belong,
And want that charm which dwells alone
Round those the fond heart calls its own,
Where, where the sunny brow?
The long-known voice – where are they now?
Thus ask I still, nor ask in vain,
The silence answers all too plain.

Oh, what is Fancy's magic worth,
If all her art cannot call forth
One bliss like those we felt of old
From lips now mute, and eyes now cold?
No, no – her spell in vain,–
As soon could she bring back again
Those eyes themselves from out the grave,
As wake again one bliss they gave.

THOMAS MOORE

SONG: TRUE LOVE LIVES IN ABSENCE

True love lives in absence,
Like angels we meet her
Dear as dreams of our childhood,
Ay, dearer and sweeter.

The words we remember
By absence unbroken
Are sweeter and dearer
Than when they were spoken.

There's a charm in the eye,
There's a smile on the face
Time, distance or trouble
Can never deface.

The pleasures of childhood
Were angels above
And the hopes of my manhood
All centred in love.

The scenes where we met,
Ay, the joys of our childhood,
There's nothing so sweet
As those fields of the wildwood

Where we met in the morning,
The noon and the gloaming
And stayed till the moon
High in heaven was roaming.

Friends meet and are happy,
So are hopes fixed above;
But there's nothing so dear
As first meetings of love.

JULIET AFTER THE MASQUERADE

*[Inspired by a Shakespearean painting of this title by
Henry Thomson, R.A.]*

She left the festival, for it seem'd dim
Now that her eye no longer dwelt on him,
And sought her chamber,– gazed (then turn'd away)
Upon a mirror that before her lay,
Half fearing, half believing her sweet face
Would surely claim within his memory place.
The hour was late, and that night her light foot
Had been the constant echo of the lute;
Yet sought she not her pillow, the cool air
Came from the casement, and it lured her there.
The terrace was beneath, and the pale moon
Shone o'er the couch which she had press'd at noon,
Soft-lingering o'er some minstrel's love-lorn page,–
Alas, tears are the poet's heritage!

She flung her on that couch, but not for sleep;
No, it was only that the wind might steep
Her fever'd lip in its delicious dew:
Her brow was burning, and aside she threw
Her cap and plume, and, loosen'd from its fold,
Came o'er her neck and face a shower of gold,
A thousand curls. It was a solitude

Made for young hearts in love's first dreaming mood:–
Beneath the garden lay, fill'd with rose-trees
Whose sighings came like passion on the breeze.
Two graceful statues of the Parian stone
So finely shaped, that as the moonlight shone
The breath of life seem'd to their beauty given,
But less the life of earth than that of heaven.
'Twas PSYCHE and her boy-god, so divine
They turn'd the terrace to an idol shrine,
With its white vases and their summer share
Of flowers, like altars raised to that sweet pair.

And there the maiden leant, still in her ear
The whisper dwelt of that young cavalier;
It was no fancy, he had named the name
Of love, and at that thought her cheek grew flame:
It was the first time her young ear had heard
A lover's burning sigh, or silver word;
Her thoughts were all confusion, but most sweet,–
Her heart beat high, but pleasant was its beat.
She murmur'd over many a snatch of song
That might to her own feelings now belong;
She thought upon old histories she had read,
And placed herself in each high heroine's stead,
Then woke her lute,– O! there is little known
Of music's power till aided by love's own.
And this is happiness: O! love will last

When all that made it happiness is past,–
When all its hopes are as the glittering toys
Time present offers, time to come destroys,–
When they have been too often crush'd to earth,
For further blindness to their little worth,–
When fond illusions have dropt one by one,
Like pearls from a rich carkanet, till none
Are left upon life's soil'd and naked string,–
And this is all what time will ever bring.
– And that fair girl,– what can the heart foresee
Of her young love, and of its destiny?
There is a white cloud o'er the moon, its form
Is very light, and yet there sleeps the storm:
It is an omen, it may tell the fate
Of love known all too soon, repented all too late.

JOURNEYS OF THE
IMAGINATION

ON FIRST LOOKING INTO
CHAPMAN'S HOMER

Much have I travell'd in the realms of gold,
And many goodly states and kingdoms seen;
Round many western islands have I been
Which bards in fealty to Apollo hold.
Oft of one wide expanse had I been told
That deep-brow'd Homer ruled as his demesne:
Yet did I never breathe its pure serene
Till I heard Chapman speak out loud and bold:
Then felt I like some watcher of the skies
When a new planet swims into his ken;
Or like stout Cortez when with eagle eyes
He star'd at the Pacific – and all his men
Look'd at each other with a wild surmise –
Silent, upon a peak in Darien.

JOHN KEATS

THE CRYSTAL CABINET

The maiden caught me in the wild,
Where I was dancing merrily;
She put me into her cabinet,
And lock'd me up with a golden key.

This cabinet is form'd of gold
And pearl and crystal shining bright,
And within it opens into a world
And a little lovely moony night.

Another England there I saw,
Another London with its Tower,
Another Thames and other hills,
And another pleasant Surrey bower,

Another maiden like herself,
Translucent, lovely, shining clear,
Threefold each in the other clos'd –
O, what a pleasant trembling fear!

O, what a smile! a threefold smile
Fill'd me, that like a flame I burn'd;
I bent to kiss the lovely maid
And found a threefold kiss return'd.

I strove to seize the inmost form
With ardour fierce and hands of flame,
But burst the crystal cabinet,
And like a weeping babe became –

A weeping babe upon the wild,
And weeping woman pale reclin'd,
And in the outward air again
I fill'd with woes the passing wind.

LA BELLE DAME SANS MERCI: A BALLAD

O what can ail thee knight at arms
  Alone and palely loitering?
The sedge has withered from the lake
  And no birds sing!

O what can ail thee knight at arms,
  So haggard and so woe begone?
The squirrel's granary is full
  And the harvest's done.

I see a lily on thy brow
  With anguish moist and fever dew,
And on thy cheeks a fading rose
  Fast withereth too –

I met a lady in the meads
  Full beautiful – a faery's child;
Her hair was long, her foot was light
  And her eyes were wild –

I made a garland for her head,
  And bracelets too, and fragrant zone;
She looked at me as she did love,
  And made sweet moan –

I set her on my pacing steed
  And nothing else saw all day long,
For sidelong would she bend, and sing
  A faery's song.

She found me roots of relish sweet
  And honey wild, and manna dew,
And sure in language strange she said
  I love thee true.

She took me to her elfin grot
  And there she wept and sigh'd full sore,
And there I shut her wild wild eyes
  With kisses four.

And there she lulled me asleep,
  And there I dream'd – Ah! Woe betide!
The latest dream I ever dreamt
  On the cold hill side.

I saw pale kings and princes too,
  Pale warriors, death pale were they all;
They cried 'La belle dame sans merci
  Thee hath in thrall.'

I saw their starv'd lips in the gloam
   With horrid warning gaped wide,
And I awoke and found me here
   On the cold hill's side.

And this is why I sojourn here
   Alone and palely loitering;
Though the sedge is wither'd from the lake,
   And no birds sing.

KUBLA KHAN
Or, a vision in a dream. A Fragment.

In Xanadu did Kubla Khan
A stately pleasure-dome decree:
Where Alph, the sacred river, ran
Through caverns measureless to man
   Down to a sunless sea.
So twice five miles of fertile ground
With walls and towers were girdled round:
And here were gardens bright with sinuous rills,
Where blossomed many an incense-bearing tree;
And here were forests ancient as the hills,
Enfolding sunny spots of greenery.

But oh! that deep romantic chasm which slanted
Down the green hill athwart a cedarn cover!
A savage place! as holy and enchanted
As e'er beneath a waning moon was haunted
By woman wailing for her demon-lover!
And from this chasm, with ceaseless turmoil seething,
As if this earth in fast thick pants were breathing,
A mighty fountain momently was forced:
Amid whose swift half-intermitted burst
Huge fragments vaulted like rebounding hail,
Or chaffy grain beneath the thresher's flail:
And 'mid these dancing rocks at once and ever

It flung up momently the sacred river.
Five miles meandering with a mazy motion
Through wood and dale the sacred river ran,
Then reached the caverns measureless to man,
And sank in tumult to a lifeless ocean:
And 'mid this tumult Kubla heard from far
Ancestral voices prophesying war!

The shadow of the dome of pleasure
Floated midway on the waves;
Where was heard the mingled measure
From the fountain and the caves.
It was a miracle of rare device,
A sunny pleasure-dome with caves of ice!

A damsel with a dulcimer
In a vision once I saw:
It was an Abyssinian maid,
And on her dulcimer she played,
Singing of Mount Abora.
Could I revive within me
Her symphony and song,
To such a deep delight 'twould win me,
That with music loud and long,
I would build that dome in air,
That sunny dome! those caves of ice!
And all who heard should see them there,

And all should cry, Beware! Beware!
His flashing eyes, his floating hair!
Weave a circle round him thrice,
And close your eyes with holy dread
For he on honey-dew hath fed,
And drunk the milk of Paradise.

from THE RIME OF THE ANCIENT
MARINER

PART THE FIRST
It is an ancient Mariner,
And he stoppeth one of three.
'By thy long grey beard and glittering eye,
Now wherefore stopp'st thou me?

The Bridegroom's doors are opened wide,
And I am next of kin;
The guests are met, the feast is set:
May'st hear the merry din.'

He holds him with his skinny hand,
'There was a ship,' quoth he.
'Hold off! unhand me, greybeard loon!'
Eftsoons his hand dropt he.

He holds him with his glittering eye –
The Wedding-Guest stood still,
And listens like a three years' child:
The Mariner hath his will.

The Wedding-Guest sat on a stone:
He cannot choose but hear;

And thus spake on that ancient man,
The bright-eyed Mariner.

'The ship was cheered, the harbour cleared,
Merrily did we drop
Below the kirk, below the hill,
Below the lighthouse top.

The Sun came up upon the left,
Out of the sea came he!
And he shone bright, and on the right
Went down into the sea.

Higher and higher every day,
Till over the mast at noon' –
The Wedding-Guest here beat his breast,
For he heard the loud bassoon.

The bride hath paced into the hall,
Red as a rose is she;
Nodding their heads before her goes
The merry minstrelsy.

The Wedding-Guest he beat his breast,
Yet he cannot choose but hear;
And thus spake on that ancient man,
The bright-eyed Mariner.

'And now the STORM-BLAST came, and he
Was tyrannous and strong:
He struck with his o'ertaking wings,
And chased us south along.

With sloping masts and dipping prow,
As who pursued with yell and blow
Still treads the shadow of his foe,
And forward bends his head,
The ship drove fast, loud roared the blast,
And southward aye we fled.

And now there came both mist and snow,
And it grew wondrous cold:
And ice, mast-high, came floating by,
As green as emerald.

And through the drifts the snowy clifts
Did send a dismal sheen:
Nor shapes of men nor beasts we ken –
The ice was all between.

The ice was here, the ice was there,
The ice was all around:
It cracked and growled, and roared and howled,
Like noises in a swound!

At length did cross an Albatross,
Thorough the fog it came;
As if it had been a Christian soul,
We hailed it in God's name.

It ate the food it ne'er had eat,
And round and round it flew.
The ice did split with a thunder-fit;
The helmsman steered us through!

And a good south wind sprung up behind;
The Albatross did follow,
And every day, for food or play,
Came to the mariners' hollo!

In mist or cloud, on mast or shroud,
It perched for vespers nine;
Whiles all the night, through fog-smoke white,
Glimmered the white Moon-shine.'

'God save thee, ancient Mariner!
From the fiends, that plague thee thus! –
Why look'st thou so?' – 'With my cross-bow
I shot the ALBATROSS.'

PART THE SECOND

'The Sun now rose upon the right:
Out of the sea came he,
Still hid in mist, and on the left
Went down into the sea.

And the good south wind still blew behind,
But no sweet bird did follow,
Nor any day for food or play
Came to the mariners' hollo!

And I had done a hellish thing,
And it would work 'em woe:
For all averred, I had killed the bird
That made the breeze to blow.
Ah wretch! said they, the bird to slay,
That made the breeze to blow!

Nor dim nor red, like God's own head,
The glorious Sun uprist:
Then all averred, I had killed the bird
That brought the fog and mist.
'Twas right, said they, such birds to slay,
That bring the fog and mist.

The fair breeze blew, the white foam flew,
The furrow followed free;

We were the first that ever burst
Into that silent sea.

Down dropt the breeze, the sails dropt down,
'Twas sad as sad could be;
And we did speak only to break
The silence of the sea!

All in a hot and copper sky,
The bloody Sun, at noon,
Right up above the mast did stand,
No bigger than the Moon.

Day after day, day after day,
We stuck, nor breath nor motion;
As idle as a painted ship
Upon a painted ocean.

Water, water, every where,
And all the boards did shrink;
Water, water, every where,
Nor any drop to drink.

The very deep did rot: O Christ!
That ever this should be!
Yea, slimy things did crawl with legs
Upon the slimy sea.

About, about, in reel and rout
The death-fires danced at night;
The water, like a witch's oils,
Burnt green, and blue and white.

And some in dreams assurèd were
Of the spirit that plagued us so;
Nine fathom deep he had followed us
From the land of mist and snow.

And every tongue, through utter drought,
Was withered at the root;
We could not speak, no more than if
We had been choked with soot.

Ah! well a-day! what evil looks
Had I from old and young!
Instead of the cross, the Albatross
About my neck was hung.

PART THE THIRD
There passed a weary time. Each throat
Was parched, and glazed each eye.
A weary time! a weary time!
How glazed each weary eye,
When looking westward, I beheld
A something in the sky.

At first it seemed a little speck,
And then it seemed a mist;
It moved and moved, and took at last
A certain shape, I wist.

A speck, a mist, a shape, I wist!
And still it neared and neared:
As if it dodged a water-sprite,
It plunged and tacked and veered.

With throats unslaked, with black lips baked,
We could nor laugh nor wail;
Through utter drought all dumb we stood!
I bit my arm, I sucked the blood,
And cried, A sail! a sail!

With throats unslaked, with black lips baked,
Agape they heard me call:
Gramercy! they for joy did grin,
And all at once their breath drew in.
As they were drinking all.

See! see! (I cried) she tacks no more!
Hither to work us weal;
Without a breeze, without a tide,
She steadies with upright keel!

The western wave was all a-flame.
The day was well nigh done!
Almost upon the western wave
Rested the broad bright Sun;
When that strange shape drove suddenly
Betwixt us and the Sun.

And straight the Sun was flecked with bars,
(Heaven's Mother send us grace!)
As if through a dungeon-grate he peered
With broad and burning face.

Alas! (thought I, and my heart beat loud)
How fast she nears and nears!
Are those *her* sails that glance in the Sun,
Like restless gossameres?

Are those *her* ribs through which the Sun
Did peer, as through a grate?
And is that Woman all her crew?
Is that a DEATH? and are there two?
Is DEATH that woman's mate?

Her lips were red, *her* looks were free,
Her locks were yellow as gold:
Her skin was as white as leprosy,

The Night-mare LIFE-IN-DEATH was she,
Who thicks man's blood with cold.

The naked hulk alongside came,
And the twain were casting dice;
"The game is done! I've won! I've won!"
Quoth she, and whistles thrice.

The Sun's rim dips; the stars rush out;
At one stride comes the dark;
With far-heard whisper, o'er the sea,
Off shot the spectre-bark.

We listened and looked sideways up!
Fear at my heart, as at a cup,
My life-blood seemed to sip!
The stars were dim, and thick the night,
The steersman's face by his lamp gleamed white;
From the sails the dew did drip –
Till clomb above the eastern bar
The hornèd Moon, with one bright star
Within the nether tip.

One after one, by the star-dogged Moon,
Too quick for groan or sigh,
Each turned his face with a ghastly pang,
And cursed me with his eye.

Four times fifty living men,
(And I heard nor sigh nor groan)
With heavy thump, a lifeless lump,
They dropped down one by one.

The souls did from their bodies fly,–
They fled to bliss or woe!
And every soul, it passed me by,
Like the whizz of my cross-bow!'

PART THE FOURTH
'I fear thee, ancient Mariner!
I fear thy skinny hand!
And thou art long, and lank, and brown,
As is the ribbed sea-sand.

I fear thee and thy glittering eye,
And thy skinny hand, so brown.'–
'Fear not, fear not, thou Wedding-Guest!
This body dropt not down.

Alone, alone, all, all alone,
Alone on a wide wide sea!
And never a saint took pity on
My soul in agony.

The many men, so beautiful!
And they all dead did lie:
And a thousand thousand slimy things
Lived on; and so did I.

I looked upon the rotting sea,
And drew my eyes away;
I looked upon the rotting deck,
And there the dead men lay.

I looked to Heaven, and tried to pray;
But or ever a prayer had gusht,
A wicked whisper came, and made
My heart as dry as dust.

I closed my lids, and kept them close,
And the balls like pulses beat;
For the sky and the sea, and the sea and the sky
Lay like a load on my weary eye,
And the dead were at my feet.

The cold sweat melted from their limbs,
Nor rot nor reek did they:
The look with which they looked on me
Had never passed away.

An orphan's curse would drag to Hell
A spirit from on high;
But oh! more horrible than that
Is the curse in a dead man's eye!
Seven days, seven nights, I saw that curse,
And yet I could not die.

The moving Moon went up the sky,
And no where did abide:
Softly she was going up,
And a star or two beside –

Her beams bemocked the sultry main,
Like April hoar-frost spread;
But where the ship's huge shadow lay,
The charmèd water burnt alway
A still and awful red.

Beyond the shadow of the ship,
I watched the water-snakes:
They moved in tracks of shining white,
And when they reared, the elfish light
Fell off in hoary flakes.

Within the shadow of the ship
I watched their rich attire:
Blue, glossy green, and velvet black,

They coiled and swam; and every track
Was a flash of golden fire.

O happy living things! no tongue
Their beauty might declare:
A spring of love gushed from my heart,
And I blessed them unaware:
Sure my kind saint took pity on me,
And I blessed them unaware.

The self-same moment I could pray;
And from my neck so free
The Albatross fell off, and sank
Like lead into the sea.'

from PETER GRIMES

[Peter Grimes in isolation after he is suspected of murdering his apprentice]

Alas! for Peter not a helping hand,
So was he hated, could he now command;
Alone he row'd his boat, alone he cast
His nets beside, or made his anchor fast;
To hold a rope or hear a curse was none,–
He toil'd and rail'd; he groan'd and swore alone.
    Thus by himself compell'd to live each day,
To wait for certain hours the tide's delay;
At the same times the same dull views to see,
The bounding marsh-bank and the blighted tree;
The water only, when the tides were high,
When low, the mud half-cover'd and half-dry;
The sun-burnt tar that blisters on the planks,
And bank-side stakes in their uneven ranks;
Heaps of entangled weeds that slowly float,
As the tide rolls by the impeded boat.
    When tides were neap, and, in the sultry day,
Through the tall bounding mud-banks made
      their way,
Which on each side rose swelling, and below
The dark warm flood ran silently and slow;
There anchoring, Peter chose from man to hide,

There hang his head, and view the lazy tide
In its hot slimy channel slowly glide;
Where the small eels that left the deeper way
For the warm shore, within the shallows play;
Where gaping mussels, left upon the mud,
Slope their slow passage to the fallen flood;—
Here dull and hopeless he'd lie down and trace
How sidelong crabs had scrawl'd their crooked race;
Or sadly listen to the tuneless cry
Of fishing gull or clanging golden-eye;
What time the sea-birds to the marsh would come,
And the loud bittern, from the bulrush home,
Gave from the salt-ditch side the bellowing boom:
He nursed the feelings these dull scenes produce,
And loved to stop beside the opening sluice;
Where the small stream, confined in narrow bound,
Ran with a dull, unvaried, sadd'ning sound;
Where all, presented to the eye or ear,
Oppress'd the soul with misery, grief, and fear.

GEORGE CRABBE   239

INTIMATIONS OF MORTALITY AND IMMORTALITY

OLD MAN TRAVELLING

       The little hedge-row birds,
That peck along the road, regard him not.
He travels on, and in his face, his step,
His gait, is one expression; every limb,
His look and bending figure, all bespeak
A man who does not move with pain, but moves
With thought – He is insensibly subdued
To settled quiet: he is one by whom
All effort seems forgotten, one to whom
Long patience has such mild composure given,
That patience now doth seem a thing, of which
He hath no need. He is by nature led
To peace so perfect, that the young behold
With envy, what the old man hardly feels.
– I asked him whither he was bound, and what
The object of his journey; he replied
'Sir! I am going many miles to take
A last leave of my son, a mariner,
Who from a sea-fight has been brought to Falmouth,
And there is dying in an hospital.'

ODE TO A NIGHTINGALE

My heart aches, and a drowsy numbness pains
  My sense, as though of hemlock I had drunk,
Or emptied some dull opiate to the drains
  One minute past, and Lethe-wards had sunk:
'Tis not through envy of thy happy lot,
  But being too happy in thine happiness,—
    That thou, light-winged Dryad of the trees,
      In some melodious plot
  Of beechen green, and shadows numberless,
    Singest of summer in full-throated ease.

O, for a draught of vintage! that hath been
  Cool'd a long age in the deep-delved earth,
Tasting of Flora and the country green,
  Dance, and Provençal song, and sunburnt mirth!
O for a beaker full of the warm South,
  Full of the true, the blushful Hippocrene,
    With beaded bubbles winking at the brim,
      And purple-stained mouth;
  That I might drink, and leave the world unseen,
    And with thee fade away into the forest dim:

Fade far away, dissolve, and quite forget
  What thou among the leaves hast never known,

The weariness, the fever, and the fret
  Here, where men sit and hear each other groan;
Where palsy shakes a few, sad, last gray hairs,
Where youth grows pale, and spectre-thin, and dies;
    Where but to think is to be full of sorrow
      And leaden-eyed despairs,
Where Beauty cannot keep her lustrous eyes,
  Or new Love pine at them beyond tomorrow.

Away! away! for I will fly to thee,
  Not charioted by Bacchus and his pards,
But on the viewless wings of Poesy,
  Though the dull brain perplexes and retards:
Already with thee! tender is the night,
  And haply the Queen-Moon is on her throne,
    Cluster'd around by all her starry Fays;
      But here there is no light,
  Save what from heaven is with the breezes blown
    Through verdurous glooms and winding
        mossy ways.

I cannot see what flowers are at my feet,
  Nor what soft incense hangs upon the boughs,
But, in embalmed darkness, guess each sweet
  Wherewith the seasonable month endows
The grass, the thicket, and the fruit-tree wild;
  White hawthorn, and the pastoral eglantine;

Fast fading violets cover'd up in leaves;
    And mid-May's eldest child,
The coming musk-rose, full of dewy wine,
    The murmurous haunt of flies on summer eves.

Darkling I listen; and, for many a time
  I have been half in love with easeful Death,
Call'd him soft names in many a mused rhyme,
    To take into the air my quiet breath;
      Now more than ever seems it rich to die,
To cease upon the midnight with no pain,
    While thou art pouring forth thy soul abroad
        In such an ecstasy!
Still wouldst thou sing, and I have ears in vain –
    To thy high requiem become a sod.

Thou wast not born for death, immortal Bird!
  No hungry generations tread thee down;
The voice I hear this passing night was heard
  In ancient days by emperor and clown:
Perhaps the self-same song that found a path
    Through the sad heart of Ruth, when, sick for home,
      She stood in tears amid the alien corn;
        The same that oft-times hath
    Charm'd magic casements, opening on the foam
      Of perilous seas, in faery lands forlorn.

Forlorn! the very word is like a bell
   To toll me back from thee to my sole self!
Adieu! the fancy cannot cheat so well
   As she is fam'd to do, deceiving elf.
Adieu! adieu! thy plaintive anthem fades
   Past the near meadows, over the still stream,
      Up the hill-side; and now 'tis buried deep
         In the next valley-glades:
   Was it a vision, or a waking dream?
      Fled is that music:– Do I wake or sleep?

THE SICK ROSE

O Rose thou art sick.
The invisible worm,
That flies in the night
In the howling storm:

Has found out thy bed
Of crimson joy:
And his dark secret love
Does thy life destroy.

THREE 'LUCY' SONGS

Strange fits of passion I have known,
And I will dare to tell,
But in the lover's ear alone,
What once to me befell.

When she I lov'd, was strong and gay
Fresh as a rose in June,
I to her cottage bent my way,
Beneath the evening moon.

Upon the moon I fix'd my eye,
All over the wide lea;
My horse trudg'd on, and we drew nigh
Those paths so dear to me.

And now we reach'd the orchard plot,
And, as we climb'd the hill,
Towards the roof of Lucy's cot
The moon descended still.

In one of those sweet dreams I slept,
Kind Nature's gentlest boon!
And, all the while, my eyes I kept
On the descending moon.

My horse mov'd on; hoof after hoof
He rais'd, and never stopp'd:
When down behind the cottage roof
At once the planet dropp'd.

What fond and wayward thoughts will slide
Into a Lover's head –
'O mercy!' to myself I cried,
'If Lucy should be dead!'

* * *

She dwelt among th' untrodden ways
   Beside the springs of Dove,
A Maid whom there were none to praise
   And very few to love:

A violet by a mossy stone
   Half-hidden from the eye!
– Fair, as a star when only one
   Is shining in the sky!

She *liv'd* unknown, and few could know
   When Lucy ceas'd to be;
But she is in her grave, and, Oh!
   The difference to me.

* * *

A slumber did my spirit seal,
　　I had no human fears:
She seem'd a thing that could not feel
　　The touch of earthly years.

No motion has she now, no force
　　She neither hears nor sees
Rolled round in earth's diurnal course
　　With rocks and stones and trees.

PROUD MAISIE

Proud Maisie is in the wood,
Walking so early;
Sweet Robin sits on the bush,
Singing so rarely.

'Tell me, thou bonny bird,
When shall I marry me?'–
'When six braw gentlemen
Kirkward shall carry ye.'

'Who makes the bridal bed,
Birdie, say truly?'–
'The gray-headed sexton
That delves the grave duly.

'The glowworm o'er grave and stone
Shall light thee steady;
The owl from the steeple sing,
"Welcome, proud lady."'

SONNET.– OZYMANDIAS

I met a traveller from an antique land
Who said: Two vast and trunkless legs of stone
Stand in the desert. Near them, on the sand,
Half sunk, a shattered visage lies, whose frown,
And wrinkled lip, and sneer of cold command,
Tell that its sculptor well those passions read
Which yet survive, stamped on these lifeless things,
The hand that mocked them and the heart that fed;

And on the pedestal these words appear:
'My name is Ozymandias, king of kings:
Look on my works, ye Mighty, and despair!'
Nothing beside remains. Round the decay
Of that colossal wreck, boundless and bare,
The lone and level sands stretch far away.

PERCY BYSSHE SHELLEY

ON A STUPENDOUS LEG OF GRANITE, DISCOVERED STANDING BY ITSELF IN THE DESERTS OF EGYPT, WITH THE INSCRIPTION INSERTED BELOW

In Egypt's sandy silence, all alone,
Stands a gigantic Leg, which far off throws
The only shadow that the Desert knows:—
'I am great OZYMANDIAS,' saith the stone,
'The King of Kings; this mighty City shows
The wonders of my hand.'— The City's gone,—
Naught but the Leg remaining to disclose
The site of this forgotten Babylon.

We wonder,— and some Hunter may express
Wonder like ours, when thro' the wilderness
Where London stood, holding the Wolf in chase,
He meets some fragment huge, and stops to guess
What powerful but unrecorded race
Once dwelt in that annihilated place.

ODE ON A GRECIAN URN

Thou still unravish'd bride of quietness,
  Thou foster-child of silence and slow time,
Sylvan historian, who canst thus express
  A flowery tale more sweetly than our rhyme:
What leaf-fring'd legend haunts about thy shape
  Of deities or mortals, or of both,
    In Tempe or the dales of Arcady?
  What men or gods are these? What maidens loth?
What mad pursuit? What struggle to escape?
  What pipes and timbrels? What wild ecstasy?

Heard melodies are sweet, but those unheard
  Are sweeter; therefore, ye soft pipes, play on;
Not to the sensual ear, but, more endear'd,
  Pipe to the spirit ditties of no tone:
Fair youth, beneath the trees, thou canst not leave
  Thy song, nor ever can those trees be bare;
    Bold Lover, never, never canst thou kiss,
Though winning near the goal – yet, do not grieve;
  She cannot fade, though thou hast not thy bliss,
    For ever wilt thou love, and she be fair!

Ah, happy, happy boughs! that cannot shed
    Your leaves, nor ever bid the Spring adieu;
And, happy melodist, unwearied,
    For ever piping songs for ever new;
More happy love! more happy, happy love!
    For ever warm and still to be enjoy'd,
        For ever panting, and for ever young;
All breathing human passion far above,
    That leaves a heart high-sorrowful and cloy'd,
        A burning forehead, and a parching tongue.

Who are these coming to the sacrifice?
    To what green altar, O mysterious priest,
Lead'st thou that heifer lowing at the skies,
    And all her silken flanks with garlands drest?
What little town by river or sea shore,
    Or mountain-built with peaceful citadel,
        Is emptied of this folk, this pious morn?
And, little town, thy streets for evermore
    Will silent be; and not a soul to tell
        Why thou art desolate, can e'er return.

O Attic shape! Fair attitude! with brede
  Of marble men and maidens overwrought,
With forest branches and the trodden weed;
  Thou, silent form, dost tease us out of thought
As doth eternity: Cold Pastoral!
  When old age shall this generation waste,
  Thou shalt remain, in midst of other woe
Than ours, a friend to man, to whom thou say'st,
  'Beauty is truth, truth beauty,'– that is all
  Ye know on earth, and all ye need to know.

JOHN KEATS

DARKNESS

I had a dream, which was not all a dream.
The bright sun was extinguish'd, and the stars
Did wander darkling in the eternal space,
Rayless, and pathless, and the icy earth
Swung blind and blackening in the moonless air;
Morn came and went – and came, and brought no day,
And men forgot their passions in the dread
Of this their desolation; and all hearts
Were chill'd into a selfish prayer for light:
And they did live by watchfires – and the thrones,
The palaces of crowned kings – the huts,
The habitations of all things which dwell,
Were burnt for beacons; cities were consumed,
And men were gather'd round their blazing homes
To look once more into each other's face;
Happy were those who dwelt within the eye
Of the volcanos, and their mountain-torch:
A fearful hope was all the world contain'd;
Forests were set on fire – but hour by hour
They fell and faded – and the crackling trunks
Extinguish'd with a crash – and all was black.
The brows of men by the despairing light
Wore an unearthly aspect, as by fits
The flashes fell upon them; some lay down
And hid their eyes and wept; and some did rest

Their chins upon their clenched hands, and smiled;
And others hurried to and fro, and fed
Their funeral piles with fuel, and look'd up
With mad disquietude on the dull sky,
The pall of a past world; and then again
With curses cast them down upon the dust,
And gnash'd their teeth and howl'd: the wild birds
    shriek'd
And, terrified, did flutter on the ground,
And flap their useless wings; the wildest brutes
Came tame and tremulous; and vipers crawl'd
And twin'd themselves among the multitude,
Hissing, but stingless – they were slain for food:
And War, which for a moment was no more,
Did glut himself again:– a meal was bought
With blood, and each sat sullenly apart
Gorging himself in gloom: no love was left;
All earth was but one thought – and that was death
Immediate and inglorious; and the pang
Of famine fed upon all entrails – men
Died, and their bones were tombless as their flesh;
The meagre by the meagre were devour'd,
Even dogs assail'd their masters, all save one,
And he was faithful to a corpse, and kept
The birds and beasts and famish'd men at bay,
Till hunger clung them, or the dropping dead
Lured their lank jaws; himself sought out no food,

But with a piteous and perpetual moan,
And a quick desolate cry, licking the hand
Which answer'd not with a caress – he died.
The crowd was famish'd by degrees; but two
Of an enormous city did survive,
And they were enemies: they met beside
The dying embers of an altar-place
Where had been heap'd a mass of holy things
For an unholy usage; they raked up,
And shivering scraped with their cold skeleton hands
The feeble ashes, and their feeble breath
Blew for a little life, and made a flame
Which was a mockery; then they lifted up
Their eyes as it grew lighter, and beheld
Each other's aspects – saw, and shriek'd, and died –
Even of their mutual hideousness they died,
Unknowing who he was upon whose brow
Famine had written Fiend. The world was void,
The populous and the powerful was a lump,
Seasonless, herbless, treeless, manless, lifeless –
A lump of death – a chaos of hard clay.
The rivers, lakes and ocean all stood still,
And nothing stirr'd within their silent depths;
Ships sailorless lay rotting on the sea,
And their masts fell down piecemeal: as they dropp'd
They slept on the abyss without a surge –
The waves were dead; the tides were in their grave,

The moon, their mistress, had expired before;
The winds were wither'd in the stagnant air,
And the clouds perish'd; Darkness had no need
Of aid from them – She was the Universe.

BRIGHT STAR

Bright star, would I were steadfast as thou art —
   Not in lone splendor hung aloft the night
And watching, with eternal lids apart,
   Like nature's patient, sleepless Eremite,
The moving waters at their priestlike task
   Of pure ablution round earth's human shores,
Or gazing on the new soft-fallen mask
   Of snow upon the mountains and the moors.
No — yet still steadfast, still unchangeable,
   Pillow'd upon my fair love's ripening breast,
To feel for ever its soft fall and swell,
   Awake for ever in a sweet unrest,
Still, still to hear her tender-taken breath,
And so live ever — or else swoon to death.

from ADONAIS: AN ELEGY ON THE DEATH
OF JOHN KEATS

Our Adonais has drunk poison – oh!
What deaf and viperous murderer could crown
Life's early cup with such a draught of woe?
The nameless worm would now itself disown:
It felt, yet could escape, the magic tone
Whose prelude held all envy, hate and wrong,
But what was howling in one breast alone,
Silent with expectation of the song,
Whose master's hand is cold, whose silver lyre
        unstrung.

Live thou, whose infamy is not thy fame!
Live! fear no heavier chastisement from me,
Thou noteless blot on a remembered name!
But be thyself, and know thyself to be!
And ever at thy season be thou free
To spill the venom when thy fangs o'erflow:
Remorse and Self-contempt shall cling to thee;
Hot Shame shall burn upon thy secret brow,
And like a beaten hound tremble thou shalt –
        as now.

Nor let us weep that our delight is fled
Far from these carrion-kites that scream below;

He wakes or sleeps with the enduring dead;
Thou canst not soar where he is sitting now.
Dust to the dust! but the pure spirit shall flow
Back to the burning fountain whence it came,
A portion of the Eternal, which must glow
Through time and change, unquenchably the same,
Whilst thy cold embers choke the sordid hearth
    of shame.

Peace, peace! he is not dead, he doth not sleep –
He hath awakened from the dream of life –
'Tis we, who lost in stormy visions, keep
With phantoms an unprofitable strife,
And in mad trance, strike with our spirit's knife
Invulnerable nothings – *We* decay
Like corpses in a charnel; fear and grief
Convulse us and consume us day by day,
And cold hopes swarm like worms within our
    living clay.

He has outsoared the shadow of our night;
Envy and calumny, and hate and pain,
And that unrest which men miscall delight,
Can touch him not and torture not again;
From the contagion of the world's slow stain
He is secure, and now can never mourn

A heart grown cold, a head grown grey in vain;
Nor, when the spirit's self has ceas'd to burn,
With sparkless ashes load an unlamented urn.

He lives, he wakes – 'tis Death is dead, not he;
Mourn not for Adonais.– Thou young Dawn,
Turn all thy dew to splendour, for from thee
The spirit thou lamentest is not gone;
Ye caverns and ye forests, cease to moan!
Cease, ye faint flowers and fountains, and thou Air,
Which like a mourning veil thy scarf hadst thrown
O'er the abandon'd Earth, now leave it bare
Even to the joyous stars which smile on its despair!

He is made one with Nature: there is heard
His voice in all her music, from the moan
Of thunder, to the song of night's sweet bird;
He is a presence to be felt and known
In darkness and in light, from herb and stone,
Spreading itself where'er that Power may move
Which has withdrawn his being to its own;
Which wields the world with never wearied love,
Sustains it from beneath, and kindles it above.

He is a portion of the loveliness
Which once he made more lovely: he doth bear

His part, while the one Spirit's plastic stress
Sweeps through the dull dense world,
    compelling there
All new successions to the forms they wear,
Torturing th' unwilling dross that checks its flight
To its own likeness, as each mass may bear;
And bursting in its beauty and its might
From trees and beasts and men into the
    heavens' light.

The splendours of the firmament of time
May be eclipsed, but are extinguished not;
Like stars to their appointed height they climb,
And death is a low mist which cannot blot
The brightness it may veil. When lofty thought
Lifts a young heart above its mortal lair,
And love and life contend in it for what
Shall be its earthly doom, the dead live there
And move like winds of light on dark and stormy air.

* * *

Go thou to Rome – at once the Paradise,
The grave, the city, and the wilderness;
And where its wrecks like shattered mountains rise,
And flowering weeds, and fragrant copses dress
The bones of Desolation's nakedness

Pass, till the spirit of the spot shall lead
Thy footsteps to a slope of green access,
Where, like an infant's smile, over the dead
A light of laughing flowers along the grass is spread

And grey walls moulder round, on which dull Time
Feeds, like slow fire upon a hoary brand;
And one keen pyramid with wedge sublime,
Pavilioning the dust of him who planned
This refuge for his memory, doth stand
Like flame transformed to marble; and beneath,
A field is spread, on which a newer band
Have pitched in Heaven's smile their camp of death,
Welcoming him we lose with scarce extinguished
    breath.

Here pause: these graves are all too young as yet
To have outgrown the sorrow which consigned
Its charge to each; and if the seal is set,
Here, on one fountain of a mourning mind,
Break it not thou! too surely shalt thou find
Thine own well full, if thou returnest home,
Of tears and gall. From the world's bitter wind
Seek shelter in the shadow of the tomb.
What Adonais is, why fear we to become?

The One remains, the many change and pass;
Heaven's light forever shines, Earth's shadows fly;
Life, like a dome of many-coloured glass,
Stains the white radiance of Eternity,
Until Death tramples it to fragments.— Die,
If thou wouldst be with that which thou dost seek!
Follow where all is fled! — Rome's azure sky,
Flowers, ruins, statues, music, words, are weak
The glory they transfuse with fitting truth to speak.

Why linger, why turn back, why shrink, my Heart?
Thy hopes are gone before: from all things here
They have departed; thou shouldst now depart!
A light is passed from the revolving year,
And man, and woman; and what still is dear
Attracts to crush, repels to make thee wither.
The soft sky smiles, the low wind whispers near:
'Tis Adonais calls! oh, hasten thither,
No more let Life divide what Death can join together.

That Light whose smile kindles the Universe,
That Beauty in which all things work and move,
That Benediction which the eclipsing Curse
Of birth can quench not, that sustaining Love
Which through the web of being blindly wove
By man and beast and earth and air and sea,
Burns bright or dim, as each are mirrors of

The fire for which all thirst, now beams on me,
Consuming the last clouds of cold mortality.

The breath whose might I have invoked in song
Descends on me; my spirit's bark is driven,
Far from the shore, far from the trembling throng
Whose sails were never to the tempest given;
The massy earth and sphered skies are riven!
I am borne darkly, fearfully, afar;
Whilst burning through the inmost veil of Heaven,
The soul of Adonais, like a star,
Beacons from the abode where the Eternal are.

ON THIS DAY I COMPLETE MY
THIRTY-SIXTH YEAR

'Tis time this heart should be unmoved,
   Since others it hath ceased to move:
Yet though I cannot be beloved,
      Still let me love!

My days are in the yellow leaf;
   The flowers and fruits of love are gone;
The worm, the canker, and the grief
      Are mine alone!

The fire that on my bosom preys
   Is lone as some volcanic isle;
No torch is kindled at its blaze –
      A funeral pile.

The hope, the fear, the jealous care,
   The exalted portion of the pain
And power of love, I cannot share,
      But wear the chain.

But 'tis not *thus* – and 'tis not *here* –
   Such thoughts should shake my soul, nor *now*,
Where glory decks the hero's bier,
      Or binds his brow.

The sword, the banner, and the field,
  Glory and Greece, around me see!
The Spartan, borne upon his shield,
    Was not more free.

Awake (not Greece – she is awake!)
  Awake, my spirit! Think through *whom*
Thy life-blood tracks its parent lake
    And then strike home!

Tread those reviving passions down,
  Unworthy manhood! – unto thee
Indifferent should the smile or frown
    Of beauty be.

If thou regret'st thy youth, *why live?*
  The land of honourable death
Is here:– up to the field, and give
    Away thy breath!

Seek out – less often sought than found –
  A soldier's grave, for thee the best;
Then look around, and choose thy ground,
    And take thy rest.

SONNET: I AM

I feel I am – I only know I am
And plod upon the earth as dull and void:
Earth's prison chilled my body with its dram
Of dullness and my soaring thoughts destroyed.
I fled to solitudes from passion's dream
But strife pursued – I only know I am.
I was a being created in the race
Of men disdaining bounds of place and time –
A spirit that could travel o'er the space
Of earth and heaven like a thought sublime,
Tracing creation, like my maker, free –
A soul unshackled – like eternity,
Spurning earth's vain and soul debasing thrall.
But now I only know I am – that's all.

LINES: I AM

I am: yet what I am none cares or knows;
  My friends forsake me like a memory lost;
I am the self-consumer of my woes –
  They rise and vanish in oblivion's host,
Like shadows in love's frenzied, stifled throes:–
  And yet I am, and live – like vapours tossed

Into the nothingness of scorn and noise,
  Into the living sea of waking dreams,
Where there is neither sense of life or joys,
  But the vast shipwreck of my life's esteems;
Even the dearest that I love the best,
  Are strange – nay, rather stranger than the rest.

I long for scenes where man hath never trod,
  A place where woman never smiled or wept –
There to abide with my Creator, God,
  And sleep as I in childhood sweetly slept,
  Untroubling and untroubled where I lie
  The grass below, above, the vaulted sky.

JOHN CLARE

SURPRISED BY JOY

Surprised by joy – impatient as the wind
I turned to share the transport – Oh! with whom
But thee, long buried in the silent tomb,
That spot which no vicissitude can find?
Love, faithful love, recalled thee to my mind –
But how could I forget thee? Through what power,
Even for the least division of an hour,
Have I been so beguiled as to be blind
To my most grievous loss? – That thought's return
Was the worst pang that sorrow ever bore,
Save one, one only, when I stood forlorn,
Knowing my heart's best treasure was no more;
That neither present time, nor years unborn
Could to my sight that heavenly face restore.

TO WORDSWORTH

Thine is a strain to read among the hills,
   The old and full of voices – by the source
Of some free stream, whose gladd'ning presence fills
   The solitude with sound; for in its course
Even such is thy deep song, that seems a part
Of those high scenes, a fountain from their heart.

Or its calm spirit fitly may be taken
   To the still breast, in sunny garden bowers,
Where vernal winds each tree's low tones awaken,
   And bud and bell with changes mark the hours.
There let thy thoughts be with me, while the day
Sinks with a golden and serene decay.

Or by some hearth where happy faces meet,
   When night hath hushed the woods, with all
       their birds,
There, from some gentle voice, that lay were sweet
   As antique music, linked with household words;
While in pleased murmurs woman's lip might move,
And the raised eye of childhood shine in love.

Or where the shadows of dark solemn yews
  Brood silently o'er some lone burial-ground,
Thy verse hath power that brightly might diffuse
  A breath, a kindling, as of spring, around;
From its own glow of hope and courage high,
And steadfast faith's victorious constancy.

True bard and holy! – thou art e'en as one
  Who, by some secret gift of soul or eye,
In every spot beneath the smiling sun,
  Sees where the springs of living waters lie;
Unseen awhile they sleep – till, touched by thee,
Bright healthful waves flow forth, to each glad
      wanderer free.

ODE: INTIMATIONS OF IMMORTALITY FROM RECOLLECTIONS OF EARLY CHILDHOOD

The child is father of the man;
And I could wish my days to be
Bound each to each by natural piety.

There was a time when meadow, grove, and stream,
The earth, and every common sight,
    To me did seem
    Apparelled in celestial light,
The glory and the freshness of a dream.
It is not now as it hath been of yore;—
    Turn wheresoe'er I may,
    By night or day,
The things which I have seen I now can see no more.

    The Rainbow comes and goes,
    And lovely is the Rose,
    The Moon doth with delight
Look round her when the heavens are bare;
    Waters on a starry night
    Are beautiful and fair;
  The sunshine is a glorious birth;
  But yet I know, where'er I go,
That there hath past away a glory from the earth.

Now, while the birds thus sing a joyous song,
  And while the young lambs bound
    As to the tabor's sound,
To me alone there came a thought of grief:
A timely utterance gave that thought relief,
    And I again am strong:
The cataracts blow their trumpets from the steep;
No more shall grief of mine the season wrong;
I hear the Echoes through the mountains throng,
The Winds come to me from the fields of sleep,
    And all the earth is gay;
      Land and sea
    Give themselves up to jollity,
     And with the heart of May
    Doth every Beast keep holiday;–
      Thou Child of Joy,
Shout round me, let me hear thy shouts, thou happy
    Shepherd-boy!

Ye blessèd creatures, I have heard the call
  Ye to each other make; I see
The heavens laugh with you in your jubilee;
  My heart is at your festival,
    My head hath its coronal,
The fulness of your bliss, I feel – I feel it all.
    Oh evil day! if I were sullen
    While Earth herself is adorning,

This sweet May-morning,
    And the Children are culling
        On every side,
    In a thousand valleys far and wide,
    Fresh flowers; while the sun shines warm,
And the Babe leaps up on his Mother's arm:—
    I hear, I hear, with joy I hear!
    — But there's a Tree, of many, one,
A single Field which I have looked upon,
Both of them speak of something that is gone:
    The Pansy at my feet
    Doth the same tale repeat:
Whither is fled the visionary gleam?
Where is it now, the glory and the dream?

Our birth is but a sleep and a forgetting:
The Soul that rises with us, our life's Star,
    Hath had elsewhere its setting,
        And cometh from afar:
    Not in entire forgetfulness,
    And not in utter nakedness,
But trailing clouds of glory do we come
    From God, who is our home:
Heaven lies about us in our infancy!
Shades of the prison-house begin to close
    Upon the growing Boy,
But he beholds the light, and whence it flows,

He sees it in his joy;
The Youth, who daily farther from the east
    Must travel, still is Nature's Priest,
    And by the vision splendid
    Is on his way attended;
At length the Man perceives it die away,
And fade into the light of common day.

Earth fills her lap with pleasures of her own;
Yearnings she hath in her own natural kind,
And, even with something of a Mother's mind,
    And no unworthy aim,
    The homely Nurse doth all she can
To make her Foster-child, her Inmate Man,
    Forget the glories he hath known,
And that imperial palace whence he came.

Behold the Child among his new-born blisses,
A six years' Darling of a pigmy size!
See, where 'mid work of his own hand he lies,
Fretted by sallies of his mother's kisses,
With light upon him from his father's eyes!
See, at his feet, some little plan or chart,
Some fragment from his dream of human life,
Shaped by himself with newly-learned art
    A wedding or a festival,
    A mourning or a funeral;

And this hath now his heart,
And unto this he frames his song:
Then will he fit his tongue
To dialogues of business, love, or strife;
But it will not be long
Ere this be thrown aside,
And with new joy and pride
The little Actor cons another part;
Filling from time to time his 'humorous stage'
With all the Persons, down to palsied Age,
That Life brings with her in her equipage;
As if his whole vocation
Were endless imitation.

Thou, whose exterior semblance doth belie
Thy Soul's immensity;
Thou best Philosopher, who yet dost keep
Thy heritage, thou Eye among the blind,
That, deaf and silent, read'st the eternal deep,
Haunted for ever by the eternal mind,–
Mighty Prophet! Seer blest!
On whom those truths do rest,
Which we are toiling all our lives to find,
In darkness lost, the darkness of the grave;
Thou, over whom thy Immortality
Broods like the Day, a Master o'er a Slave,
A Presence which is not to be put by;

Thou little Child, yet glorious in the might
Of heaven-born freedom on thy being's height,
Why with such earnest pains dost thou provoke
The years to bring the inevitable yoke,
Thus blindly with thy blessedness at strife?
Full soon thy Soul shall have her earthly freight,
And custom lie upon thee with a weight,
Heavy as frost, and deep almost as life!

   O joy! that in our embers
   Is something that doth live,
   That Nature yet remembers
   What was so fugitive!
The thought of our past years in me doth breed
Perpetual benediction: not indeed
For that which is most worthy to be blest;
Delight and liberty, the simple creed
Of Childhood, whether busy or at rest,
With new-fledged hope still fluttering in his breast:–
   Not for these I raise
   The song of thanks and praise
  But for those obstinate questionings
  Of sense and outward things,
  Fallings from us, vanishings;
  Blank misgivings of a Creature
Moving about in worlds not realised,
High instincts before which our mortal Nature

Did tremble like a guilty Thing surprised:
    But for those first affections,
    Those shadowy recollections,
  Which, be they what they may,
Are yet the fountain light of all our day,
Are yet a master light of all our seeing;
    Uphold us, cherish, and have power to make
Our noisy years seem moments in the being
Of the eternal Silence: truths that wake,
    To perish never;
Which neither listlessness, nor mad endeavour,
    Nor Man nor Boy,
Nor all that is at enmity with joy,
Can utterly abolish or destroy!
    Hence in a season of calm weather
    Though inland far we be,
Our Souls have sight of that immortal sea
    Which brought us hither,
  Can in a moment travel thither,
And see the Children sport upon the shore,
And hear the mighty waters rolling evermore.

Then sing, ye Birds, sing, sing a joyous song!
    And let the young Lambs bound
    As to the tabor's sound!
We in thought will join your throng,
    Ye that pipe and ye that play,

          Ye that through your hearts to-day
               Feel the gladness of the May!
What though the radiance which was once so bright
Be now for ever taken from my sight,
          Though nothing can bring back the hour
Of splendour in the grass, of glory in the flower;
               We will grieve not, rather find
               Strength in what remains behind;
               In the primal sympathy
               Which having been must ever be;
               In the soothing thoughts that spring
               Out of human suffering;
               In the faith that looks through death,
In years that bring the philosophic mind.

And O, ye Fountains, Meadows, Hills, and Groves,
Forebode not any severing of our loves!
Yet in my heart of hearts I feel your might;
I only have relinquished one delight
To live beneath your more habitual sway.
I love the Brooks which down their channels fret,
Even more than when I tripped lightly as they;
The innocent brightness of a new-born Day
               Is lovely yet;
The Clouds that gather round the setting sun
Do take a sober colouring from an eye
That hath kept watch o'er man's mortality;

Another race hath been, and other palms are won.
Thanks to the human heart by which we live,
Thanks to its tenderness, its joys, and fears,
To me the meanest flower that blows can give
Thoughts that do often lie too deep for tears.

AN INVITE TO ETERNITY

Wilt thou go with me sweet maid
Say maiden wilt thou go with me
Through the valley-depths of shade
Of night and dark obscurity
Where the path hath lost its way
Where the sun forgets the day
Where there's nor life nor light to see
Sweet maiden wilt thou go with me

Where stones will turn to flooding streams,
Where plains will rise like ocean waves,
Where life will fade like visioned dreams
And mountains darken into caves
Say maiden wilt thou go with me
Through this sad non-identity
Where parents live and are forgot
And sisters live and know us not

Say maiden wilt thou go with me
In this strange death of life to be
To live in death and be the same
Without this life or home or name
At once to be and not to be
That was and is not – yet to see

Things pass like shadows – and the sky
Above, below, around us lie

The land of shadows wilt thou trace
And look nor know each other's face
The present mixed with seasons gone
And past, and present all as one
Say maiden can thy life be led
To join the living with the dead
Then trace thy footsteps on with me
We're wed to one eternity

JOHN CLARE

POETS

William Blake (1757–1827)
Robert Burns (1759–1796)
George Gordon, Lord Byron (1788–1824)
John Clare (1793–1864)
Samuel Taylor Coleridge (1772–1834)
William Cowper (1731–1800)
George Crabbe (1754–1832)
Felicia Hemans (1793–1835)
Leigh Hunt (1784–1859)
John Keats (1795–1821)
Letitia Elizabeth ('L. E. L.') Landon (1802–1838)
Thomas Moore (1779–1852)
Hannah More (1745–1833)
Mary Robinson (1757–1800)
Samuel Rogers (1763–1855)
Sir Walter Scott (1771–1832)
Percy Bysshe Shelley (1792–1822)
Charlotte Smith (1749–1806)
Horace Smith (1779–1849)
Robert Southey (1774–1843)
Helen Maria Williams (1759–1827)
Dorothy Wordsworth (1771–1855)
William Wordsworth (1770–1850)